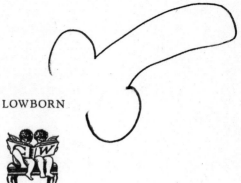

LOWBORN

*Tony Hogan Bought Me an Ice-cream
Float Before He Stole My Ma*
Thirst

KERRY HUDSON

LOWBORN

Growing Up, Getting Away and Returning to Britain's Poorest Towns

Sylvie,
These boobs are all my
responsibility!

Chatto & Windus
LONDON

5 7 9 10 8 6

Chatto & Windus, an imprint of Vintage,
20 Vauxhall Bridge Road,
London SW1V 2SA

Chatto & Windus is part of the Penguin Random House group of companies
whose addresses can be found at global.penguinrandomhouse.com.

Penguin
Random House
UK

First published in the United Kingdom by Chatto & Windus in 2019

penguin.co.uk/vintage

A CIP catalogue record for this book is available from the British Library

ISBN 9781784742454

Typeset in 11/15pt Goudy Old Style by Jouve (UK), Milton Keynes
Printed and bound in Great Britain by Clays Ltd, Elcograf S.p.A.

Penguin Random House is committed to a sustainable future
for our business, our readers and our planet. This book is made
from Forest Stewardship Council® certified paper.

LOWBORN

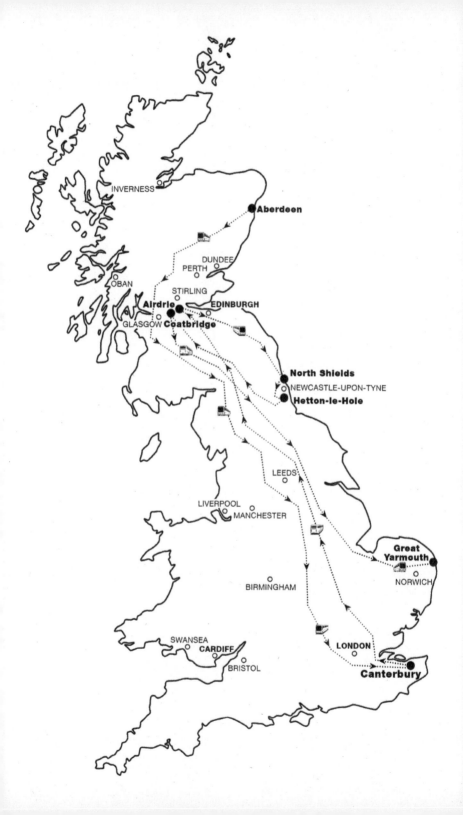

INVERNESS

● **Aberdeen**

DUNDEE
PERTH

OBAN

STIRLING
Airdrie
EDINBURGH
GLASGOW **Coatbridge**

● **North Shields**
○ NEWCASTLE-UPON-TYNE
● **Hetton-le-Hole**

LEEDS

LIVERPOOL
MANCHESTER

● **Great Yarmouth**
NORWICH

BIRMINGHAM

SWANSEA
CARDIFF
BRISTOL

LONDON

● **Canterbury**

For all of you who have lived this story too.

Contents

Note from the Author

This is my story told as well as I can tell it. Though I have changed names, physical and other distinguishing details where necessary, I have presented everything as honestly as I can, based on my own memory, anecdote and, where possible, official documentation. Like any memoir, it is subject to human error and I acknowledge that this is my account of events and that there may be many different perspectives and that this is simply mine told in my own way.

Introduction

Shall we start with a happy ending? I made it. I rose. I escaped poverty. I escaped bad food because that's all you can afford. I escaped threadbare clothes and too-tight shoes. I escaped drinking or drugging myself into oblivion because . . . because. I probably escaped the early mortality rates and preventable diseases – we'll see. I escaped obesity. I escaped the higher rate of domestic abuse. I escaped sink estates, burnt-out houses and ice-cream vans selling drugs at the school gates. I escaped Jeremy Kyle in a shiny suit telling me my sort was scum. I escaped casual, grim violence fuelled by frustration and Special Brew. I escaped benefits queues and means assessments and shitty zero-hour contracts. I escaped hopelessness.

I lived more of that life, my first twenty years, than I've lived of this infinitely cushier one since. And the names still ring in my head every day: chav, scav, lowlife, NED, underclass, lowborn.

Yes, I might have been lowborn but, somehow, I ascended. I reached up high enough to write these words and believe someone might read them. Now I eat well and always have somewhere decent to stay. My clothes are cheap, but I can afford to replace them. I enjoy the luxury of exercise. I heat my flat in the winter. I have access to art, music, film, books and they don't feel like a foolishness. When I've been unwell, in mind or body, I've sought help, it's been given, and I've got better. I've travelled the world several times over and made a living doing what I love which also happens to be the preserve of People Not Like Me.

But now let's go back to the beginning:

1 single mother
2 stays in foster care
9 primary schools
1 sexual abuse child protection inquiry
5 high schools
2 sexual assaults
1 rape
2 abortions
My 18th birthday

The Adverse Childhood Experiences questionnaire asks ten questions to measure childhood trauma and each affirmative answer gives you a point. Research has shown that an individual with an ACE score of 4 or higher is '260% more likely to have chronic obstructive pulmonary disease than someone with a score of 0, 240% more likely to contract hepatitis, 460% more likely to experience depression, and 1,220% more likely to attempt suicide'. I scored 8.

It might be easier to believe that I was somehow unlucky. That I was a terrible exception. But the truth is the people I grew up with experienced much the same. A little less sometimes. Often a lot more. The difference for me? I saw something on the horizon and I ran. I ran, and I never looked over my shoulder.

I am proudly working class and, in this socially mobile hinterland I currently occupy, I miss the sense of community and belonging which that tribe might provide me.

But I was never proudly poor. True poverty is all-encompassing, grinding, brutal and often dehumanising. I think it goes without saying that the gnawing shame and fear of poverty is not something I have ever missed, particularly since I frequently still experience its aftershocks.

While my life is unrecognisable today, I find myself unable to reconcile my 'now' with my past. I can best describe this vertiginous feeling as belonging nowhere and to no one, neither 'back there' nor truly 'here'. I have come to believe that being born poor is not simply a matter of economics or situation, it is a psychology and identity all its own that, in me, has endured well beyond my 'escape'.

This book is the outcome of the questions that still disturb my peace. What happened to those towns I lived in? Surely things got better? There are other questions too, less easy to confront out loud, except perhaps when I wake up at night screaming obscenities at phantom shapes, inky terror running through me. What happened to me during those years? Have I really escaped? Has my fragmented memory been protecting me all these years or has it inflated, year by year, this terror? How much of my past is still part of who I am today?

A year ago, I realised I could only really answer these questions if I went back. If I looked my monster in the face in the hope it would only be a shadow, after all.

I decided to go back to Aberdeen where I was born into a clan of matriarchal fishwives and follow the staggering, itinerant route of my childhood down the country: Aberdeen, Canterbury, North Lanarkshire, Sunderland, Great Yarmouth. Not so different from my ancestors chasing herring, silver darlings, down the line of the coast, but I would be casting my net for stories and facts, then I'd cut them open and see what the guts told me.

Did those towns die with the decline of their traditional industries? What was it like to be poor or working class and living there now? What did working class even mean any more? If I was a child or a teen growing up there today would there be hope?

Who lives where I used to? What about the kids on the streets? I planned to simply ask those questions to people going about their daily business, and to those working on the front line of austerity and at grass-roots level, people new to those towns and people who'd lived there for decades, to see how these communities were living and surviving – or not.

As I went up and down the country I'd retrace my own child-hood and try to fill the gaping holes in my memory by requesting my child protection documents, medical and school records, by hunting down anyone who might remember who I was. Anyone who could maybe remind me, too.

I decided to seek answers to my questions because, now, I believed I could open my mouth to ask and not be punched or punished or ridiculed. Because my happy ending needed to be tested so I could sleep through the night. Because, if it *was* a happy ending, I should care about what I left behind. I should stop, look over my shoulder and understand what I came from.

When every day of your life you have been told you have nothing of value to offer, that you are worth nothing to society, can you ever escape that sense of being 'lowborn' no matter how far you've come?

1
Aberdeen
1980

My mum was twenty when she met my dad. She'd left Aberdeen at sixteen with no qualifications, then travelled about the UK working as a waitress, spending her spare time and her tips at discos. She always called herself the black sheep of the family. But when I once repeated that to my grandma, she arched an eyebrow and said in her terrifyingly slow, low voice, 'Oh, she says that, does she?'

Everything I knew about Mum I learned from the stories she told me herself. In the course of writing this book I would learn more, more perhaps than I'd wish to, but when I was a child she told me how much she loved dancing. She adored Blondie, Bowie and Leonard Cohen and reminiscing about a particular sheer, sparkling silver dress she'd wear to nightclubs in London, and how everyone would watch her as she walked to the bar. She had a huge laugh, as all of the women in our family did, bellowing and dirty and full of irrepressible life, no matter how hard life tried to repress her.

But she was also extremely, possibly irretrievably, vulnerable and fractured, and extraordinarily naive. She was proud of our tough fishwife heritage and was a feminist before she knew the word. She had been, one relative told me, 'shy and giggly' as a teen but then went to London and found her confidence away from her mother who she had a very difficult relationship with. She had certain absolutely unyielding moral values: women weren't lesser than men, you should never ever be racist, never kick a dog when it's down.

My father was forty-two when he met my mother. He was not

yet a diagnosed schizophrenic or Valium addict, but he was receiving a pension from the US Army after a breakdown during basic training twenty-six years before and was already in the grip of alcoholism.

Dad had an unpredictable relationship with the truth, but I will tell you, anyway, the stories he told me about where he came from. He said that one side of our family had owned half of California, until my great-grandmother ran away and married a cotton picker. That he lived with various relatives before ending up in a boys' home in South Central LA. In some stories he was the only white kid, in others not. At sixteen he'd gone straight into the army, but then he'd had his nervous breakdown and ended up spending three years, maybe more, in a German mental hospital.

After discharge, he told me, he returned to California, went briefly to UCLA but never graduated, worked as a mailman and once chatted to Charlie Manson on the stoop of a house, hung around with the beatniks at City Lights in San Francisco (one of the poets, I forget which one, stole his wineskin and he was still sore about it decades later), got married to a beautiful Japanese woman who broke his heart, was scouted by a model agency and eventually washed up in London.

It's not hard for me to see why these two people, both orphans in their own way, transient and looking for escapism, might temporarily find solace in their own strangely distorted reflection. But it's impossible to imagine it might have lasted.

They can't have been together more than a few months. My mum always used to talk about that time, her last burst of freedom before me. She told me they drank Brandy Alexanders, lived in a squat and embraced the party life of late-seventies London. My dad even took my mum on an impromptu trip to America. They arrived with almost no money so set off from San Francisco to visit my grandmother, who was living in a trailer in San Diego, to see if she might help them out. My mother was cleaning her feet in my paternal grandmother's sink when they first met. Later, my father went through his mother's meagre jewellery box for something to pawn while my grandmother watched on.

By the time they got the money together to fly back to London my mum was pregnant with me. They had fully embraced the hedonism of the West Coast scene and I still wonder if that explains this strong imagination of mine. Soon after they arrived back in London my mum told my dad she was pregnant. When he fell to his knees and cried, 'What am I going to do?' my mum broke up with him and booked an appointment at an abortion clinic.

She was twenty, vulnerable and jobless, and I don't doubt an abortion would probably have been the best thing for her. She told me often – several times each year – how she'd booked the appointment and was on the Tube to the clinic and then changed her mind.

I don't think she was telling the story to be cruel. I believe she was trying to tell me that she'd chosen me. That I'd been an accident but then I'd been a decision. That no matter how bad things were, at least I was alive when I might not have been. But she also told me that, though she loved me, having me had meant she had sacrificed her whole life. There is a strange, nauseous pull in knowing that that decision had made both our lives so much worse.

And so, she travelled back to Aberdeen, to a place she'd never wanted to return to, that she couldn't get away from fast enough. She returned to her mother, my grandma, the very picture of an Aberdonian working-class matriarch.

My grandma was the most terrifying woman I've ever known.

She could be charming, loving even, but if crossed, you'd see her become very still, her speech would slow, her manicured finger point towards you, eyes like ice. As a child she once demanded the biggest Easter egg in the shop from my great-grandad and then smashed it over his head during a temper tantrum on the bus home. In her teens, Grandma had looked like Elizabeth Taylor. She had violet eyes and her body had bloomed so abundantly and so unexpectedly that one time she even shattered her teeth on the rocks of the Bay of Nigg diving in to hide herself from the stares of boys. In her last days she refused everything except her Lambrini and fags, knowing full well she was killing herself.

She spent her whole life in the fish houses, like every woman before her in the family. It was a job of brutal conditions and vicious workplace politics. She often described how fast she was with her filleting knife, how her hands would go blue and crack from the cold. Her favourite story to entertain me with as a wee girl was about a group of women who wanted her better paid filleting position and were making her life a misery. One day one of them called her a cunt, and, she told me in that low, slow, furious tone of hers, 'I held my knife right to her throat and said to her, "I'm a good *cunt*, a clean *cunt*, and I care a *cunt* for no *cunt*, right, *cunt*?"'

She told me all the time, 'Don't let the dogs get you down.'

She told me to always stick up for myself.

She told me to grab the hair first in fights, to use my nails.

With no other options, my pregnant mum moved back in with Grandma and started work in the fish factory as a packer. I've often imagined the heavy apron over her swollen belly, the metallic-smelling air a mix of sea and blood. She told me how on Fridays, payday, she and the other women had fish suppers on their lunch break and afterwards she'd go into town and buy a little thing for me from Mothercare – a tiny pair of yellow socks, perhaps a Babygro. My grandma knitted the rest for me, little bootees and crotchet jumpers. I suspect my great-aunties and great-grandma did too.

Mum always spoke about the time carrying me as though she was keeping some sort of happy secret. I suppose once she'd decided to have me she was optimistic about there being someone to love and receiving uncomplicated love in return. It must have been easy to overlook all the ways that she was not ready to be a mother.

My mum and grandma were watching *The House That Dripped Blood* when, two weeks late, I started to demand release. Mum refused to go to hospital until the end of the film and I can conjure her there, sitting grim-faced, gripping the arms of Grandma's old mint velour sofa, probably smoking a fag, stubbornly refusing to accept that her life was about to change, her and Grandma rowing. Still, I came, screaming into the world, whether Mum was ready or not.

When Grandma held me for the first time she looked at me and declared, 'She's like a wee pound of Kerrygold Butter.' Soon enough, 'Kerrygold' was shortened to Kerry and that was the name that appeared on my birth certificate. Date of birth: 12 October 1980. Mother: Fiona Mackie. Father: Unknown.

It's hard enough to imagine how those two strong, complex women with their history of rows had managed, stewing away in that tiny Aberdeen flat, during the long months of my mum's pregnancy. But it seems that when I actually arrived I was one ingredient too many for that highly combustible mix. A few weeks after I came home, for one reason or another, my mum and I ended up living in a women's refuge. Mum always spoke about it fondly, as though we'd been on a holiday. I can see how it might have felt like that for her – the emotional and practical support, a community of women who understood what it was to be beaten down, tired, and yet wake every day still fighting.

There was only one baby photo of me, one record of me, during this time. Chubby and naked, the sepia tinting my blue eyes grey. I lay on a white mat covered in orange flowers. I was a surprisingly fat baby, arms and legs raised, looking away from the camera.

I used to take out that picture a lot when I was a kid. As a teen, I still occasionally took it out, though it was creased and tattered by that time, trying to work out how much of me was in that baby, or perhaps enjoying the sight of that tot who didn't know what lay ahead. The photo got torn up by Mum in one of our last rows in my mid-twenties. But whenever I think about myself brand new, I see those sepia colours and I think of that fat little baby who didn't want to show her face to the camera.

2
Hue
2017

Six months into a trip around the world together, in the second year of our relationship, I took Peter, my boyfriend, to see 'my' Vietnam. I say 'mine' because it is where I wrote my first novel, *Tony Hogan Bought Me an Ice-Cream Float Before He Stole My Ma*, a semi-fictionalised version of my childhood that enabled me to lay at least a few ghosts to rest as I frantically purged my story into school exercise books during the rainy season.

In Hue, a small fortress town, I showed Peter the cafe where, seven years earlier, I'd written those first chapters by hand, typing them up later at an Internet cafe full of smoke, boys playing video games and men watching YouTube videos of schoolgirls fighting.

There are pictures of our visit to Hue, eating pineapple rice, drinking *ca phe sua da* from plastic cups under a willow tree by the murky river, me hunched over my notebook in a restaurant garden that had been filled with the sound of frogs. Walking to the fortress I used to cycle around, watching two little girls crouched over a baby bird with slick feathers, feeding it some sort of bloody mush with a tiny silver spoon. I look so happy in those photos.

One night I had a slight bug and we stayed in the guest house watching an American procedural drama with the remnants of our dinner of club sandwiches around us as I idly checked my Facebook. A new friend request from Mark Mackie. I didn't recognise the name at first and I almost declined the request. It took moments, my brain turning on itself, before my mind connected that name with me, my genes, the past. Before the memory of that name and face assimilated.

'Oh my God. It's my uncle. Uncle Mark.' Then I started crying.

My Facebook profile represents the strange life I now occupy. 818 of my closest friends. Among them, a range of French literati and an Italian lit gang, my Ivy League students from my summers teaching creative writing at Cambridge. Old colleagues from my eight years working for NGOs and my artsy queer pals. A scattering of kind people I'd met only once or twice at conferences or festivals in Korea, Japan, Croatia, Australia and the US. Peter's friends and family, and the family of my ex-partner, Susanna. In short, various overlapping circles, a Venn diagram of the life I live now, with me in various fragments at the centre.

But there was no circle for who I was for the first two decades of my life. Not until Uncle Mark showed up there. Someone I hadn't seen for twenty-three years.

Peter, in his usual steadying way, already had his arm around my sweaty shoulder. 'Are you happy?'

It wasn't that he didn't know about my childhood. In the early tumult of our relationship I'd told him about my family to help him understand me, my fears, my barriers, my need for love that feels like a solid, immovable thing. He knew anxiety gnawed at me, a big black dog with a bone. He knew I didn't speak to my family and how sad that made me and also that it was the only way it could be.

But I don't blame him for not understanding that hearing from a long-lost relative might not, in fact, be a good thing. Peter comes from an upper-middle-class family, who are close-knit and supportive of one another. He spent his early years living in a Swiss mansion near Zurich, he went to International School. His upbringing was not like my upbringing. His family was not like my family. Sometimes, when talking about my childhood, it felt like I was translating, as though we were from entirely different cultures. Because of course we were.

I am not a still person. I am always moving, talking, doing. Mum always said I was a 'fidget Annie'. But for a few seconds I stared at the screen absolutely still. 'You know, my family . . . I just hope this doesn't blow up in my face.'

I clicked 'accept'.

'Well, you've done it in good faith. You can always unfriend him again.'

An hour later there was a post, sandwiched between a picture I'd taken of cats and an article about the Glasgow Women's Library. Squeezed into the life I'd carefully chosen – curated no less – was a message from my Uncle Mark. 'Kerry you my friend now on face book.'

I'm ashamed that I wanted to delete it. I imagined what people would think. That disjointed sentence linking me to a man whose last post had been a meme about illegal immigrants claiming £29,900 of benefits and how it was 'bloody disgusting'.

His profile picture was unrecognisable as the cocky, handsome, auburn-haired twenty-year-old I'd known, with his swagger and freckles and the genetic raucous family laugh. He was broader, wearing thick-lensed glasses, a yellow T-shirt and a baseball hat. My mum stood behind him.

Over a decade ago I made the painful but wholly necessary decision to estrange myself from my mum. Perhaps inevitably this has meant I have become estranged from the rest of my close family, too. I did not remove myself from her because I did not love her. I did it because I loved her so deeply that whatever she did affected me just as deeply. Especially if it was incomprehensible and irrational. And it so often was.

In the end, I removed myself because I could not live with the rages and denial of the past. I didn't want an apology. I understand well enough that apologies only come when there is blame, and there is no one to blame for the hardship of my childhood. But I did need someone to say 'yes, that happened and that was shitty'. I did it because it seemed the only other option would mean sacrificing my own sanity and that wasn't a price I was willing to pay. I did it because I had felt I was finally swimming towards something brighter, but my family, whether it was out of love or not, kept coiling themselves around my ankles, pulling me down, filling my mouth with the filthy water.

Tearing myself away both breaks my heart and is the only thing that has kept me intact, if often only barely.

I have only seen one or two photos of Mum since cutting contact. There, in that faraway place, I studied her face. She looked like my mum. She looked like me. She looked like a stranger. A few more wrinkles, her teeth strong like mine are. Her eyes were wide, her mouth grinning.

I was deeply moved and also horrified to see all that in the photo on my own Facebook wall. It felt as though my mum and uncle had marched into that airless room in a foreign land where I thought I was safe and demanded an audience. I wrote under Mark's post, 'I'll send you a private message.' He replied with a story about how when I was a kid, me and another toddler stripped down and painted each other from head to toe with white gloss paint. I'd forgotten it entirely but as soon as I read it, I remembered: the smell of the turps, the rubbing of my skin pink and raw like a prawn penny sweet, everyone laughing their heads off at our mischief.

I wondered how many other memories were stored away,

waiting for a single badly written sentence to unravel them, and what it would be like if I allowed that past to become some of my present. How could this life, the one I'd chosen and strived for, be truly real if it had none of my first twenty years in it?

That evening I felt something building, fizzing up the way sherbet does when it hits a drop of moisture. Agitating, expanding. I was tired. I usually was. I'd been having night terrors – waking, hyperrealistic nightmares – every night for months. I'd had them since childhood. In those months travelling with Peter they'd been worse and more vivid than ever before. I woke to find men with skinheads looming over me, or shotguns pointed at my head, small children standing, terrified, by the side of my bed begging for help I couldn't give. Peter had learned to hold me through the screaming, crying and struggling, repeating, 'It's OK, I'm here.'

It wasn't until the lights were off and the room was completely black that I allowed myself to reach out for Peter. 'I'm so frightened.'

He pulled me to him, I put my head on his chest and curled myself around him just as a child would.

'What are you frightened of?'

'Everything I can't remember.'

And then I talked and cried and held myself to him like he was the only thing keeping my limbs together until the wee hours of the morning.

That night, because I was a little sick and tired and in that strange, damp-smelling windowless room, all the questions I had never fully asked myself began. Why, I asked him, was I so frightened all the time? Had something been done to me? Why hadn't anyone helped us? How can you ever become a grown-up with a childhood like that?

I knew I'd been taken into foster homes, could remember tiny fragments. I have one clear memory of one of the homes – the largest, cleanest kitchen I'd ever seen, me on a counter, my mum coming to visit me, skinnier than ever and still black-eyed, crying, asking me if I wanted her to look after me again. I don't remember the foster-carer but somehow over the years she's morphed into the Bisto mum. I don't know why none of my great-aunts, great-uncles or grandma, who'd all seemed so charmed by me when they were drinking and telling stories, didn't take me. I don't understand why they let me just go and live with strangers. And, I don't remember anything that happened in those foster homes. Maybe nothing at all but meals with good gravy and a gentle, normal home life.

But not knowing is scary and that night in that guest-house room, with a man who I knew loved me, in a place so far from Aberdeen, I finally allowed myself to be that frightened child.

Three days later we'd take motorbike taxis up a thrillingly treacherous mountain pass in northern Vietnam and Peter would propose at the top of the world. We'd celebrate with our motorbike taxi drivers and a man who ran a shack of a cafe right at the edge of the mountain. I had never felt so safe or loved. And I was terrified I'd never be well enough to deserve it.

So I decided I would make that terrible night, and the good life I had built myself, mean something. Then I got word my publisher wanted me to write this book. It was time to turn round, face my past and fears, and simply accept that walking backwards might just cause some broken bones.

3
Aberdeen
1981

The first council flat Mum and I lived in was on Manor Avenue, right at the edge of a rough estate miles away from Torry and the rest of the family. It was a bleak, hulking granite block of a house with four flats. Ours had a big fireplace but it was given to us unfurnished – as if people like my mum could find the money to just go out and buy furniture, a newborn in tow, and get it into the house by herself.

Even though we had visitors in that house, what I remember most is how vast and empty the rooms seemed. It felt like it was only me and my mum, we were alone in the world, and that world was a fearful place.

Other memories are sparse: a plastic bath by a roaring fire; the cold and damp; my mum pulling an enormous chest of drawers across the door to the bedroom to lock me inside and me screaming and screaming for her, and, when she didn't come, deliberately shitting myself in outrage.

My mum used to tell me about the time I gave my Uncle Mark a little lump of my shit to show him how good I was at the potty and him almost eating it, thinking it was a Malteser. Or the time I poured instant coffee into the toaster to make my mum coffee or filled the bathtub with coal to make her a bath.

Even back then, literally before memory, I knew my mum needed caring for.

When I was a few months old my father came to see me. It's almost impossible to imagine my father in Aberdeen. A tall American but so unlike the flashy, macho 'Yanks' in Aberdeen for the oil business. As I'd discover from my later encounters with him, he was a man who wore army coats, listened to Chet Baker, did bad pen sketches in little notebooks while sitting in cafes, spoke about all the things he had the talent to do but hadn't pursued. Even when on the wagon, he was prone to outbursts which would turn his gentle, slightly flamboyant personality nasty.

I can't marry the idea of him and his carefully crafted artistic persona with wandering the grim streets around Manor Avenue.

We met up in a cafe in town. It was winter. I imagine a cosy cafe of my childhood, yellow Formica tables, cigarette smoke and steamy warmth from the coffee machine. It would sell pale, fatty bacon and toasted teacakes burnt around the edges.

My mum often described the scene, how I was all wrapped up in a snowsuit, a baby Michelin Man. She said she sat me on the table between them and then pushed me towards him. 'I can't do this. You take her.'

My dad, who was probably drunk and would definitely have been stoned, pushed me back. 'I can't look after a child. I never wanted to bring a child into this world.'

Mum pushed me towards him again and he returned me. Mum said I was good while this was going on, that I thought it was some sort of game. Baby ping-pong. This was often repeated as a funny story. But I never found it quite as funny as everyone else.

My father went back to London not to be seen for another few years. My mum was left with me and I was left with her.

There are more interwoven stories and memories. How cold the flat on Manor Avenue would get. How Mum would stroke my little button nose to get me off to sleep and sing to me 'If I had a hammer, I'd hammer out a warning . . .'

As often as she told me about how she'd booked the

appointment to abort me or how neither she nor my dad wanted me, she told me how much she loved me, how it was just the two of us in the whole world, how she'd die for me.

Of course, domestic violence happens across the social and economic spectrum. But my mum was a prime candidate. She was young, unsupported by her family, already in a bad situation, had a deep mistrust of the authorities, no money to go anywhere and no one to turn to.

His face is one of my first clear memories. I struggle to remember whole months of my childhood and youth. I don't remember what my auntie or great-grandma or even what the boy I lost my virginity to looked like in any detail. But Jimmy, my first 'uncle', I remember in crystal detail.

He dyed his hair a flat blue-black, must have spent so much time each morning spiking it with gel. It didn't go well with his pink complexion that turned a deeper shade when he was angry. He wore tight double denim and gold chains like many men at the time. In the early eighties, he would have probably been considered good-looking, *Lost Boys*-ish. He had nunchucks, the martial arts weapon, two blocks of wood connected by a thick chain. He thought himself a real hard man, an Aberdonian Bruce Lee. And wanted me and Mum to know that too.

He'd stand in his vest, flexing his muscles, face smiling, focused, back straight, swinging the nunchucks faster and faster in a figure of eight as though he was onstage and not in our dreary bedroom with its stained carpet.

Then he'd start stepping towards us, his smile getting wider and the wooden blocks coming closer, so we could feel the air whipping them inches from our heads. Backed against the wall, if we'd moved a muscle our faces would have been smashed by the force of them. As he did this, his face flitted through moods: delighted;

amused by us; deadly fucking serious. Almost like the showman-ship of a knife thrower at the circus except our terrified cries were absolutely real.

He bought me some child-sized nunchucks and encouraged me to do the same in Mum's face. And I'm ashamed to say I did, him egging me on, until Mum begged me crying to stop and I ran to hide in her arms while he loomed over us furious at my betrayal, the nunchucks still slicing the air a few millimetres from our heads.

Mum had no money, I was now a toddler and she'd nowhere to run.

It was around this time that I dared the boy next door to go across the absolutely forbidden main road and he got run over and broke his leg. I killed all my goldfish with a seaside spade. I took to squashing worms I'd dug up from the scrappy front yard between two pieces of abandoned wood. I believed I was evil.

I don't know how long Jimmy was with us. How long it was three of us instead of two. He stopped living with us after my mum dragged me out of bed in the middle of the night and out onto our front-door steps, screaming to the neighbourhood, 'He's going to kill us. He'll kill me and my kid,' holding me with one hand and him pulling us back by the other. But we lived on Manor Avenue, where everyone had enough problems of their own. The curtains stayed closed, the lights stayed off and he dragged us inside again. I don't remember anything else about that night.

The last time I saw him was years later, when we had been rehomed onto another estate in another part of Aberdeen. Mum and him got drunk and she dared me to put some of my ice cream on his face. I smashed the whole ice cream cone onto his nose and then held my breath while Mum laughed and laughed, and he quivered with barely contained rage.

It was my first taste of fighting back.

4
Liverpool
2017

When we returned to the UK we chose to live in Liverpool for no better reason than it was not London and not Scotland, neither of which we could agree on. There, we hoped, we'd find work and a sense of home.

Perhaps appropriately, the large but cheap one-bedroom garden flat was smack between Toxteth, one of Liverpool's most deprived areas still famous for its 1981 riots, and the gentrified Lark Lane, full of vintage shops and hipster bars. We arrived by taxi to an entirely empty flat and sat and ate takeaway bacon sandwiches on the floor by our travel-beaten rucksacks.

Over the coming weeks, I filled the flat with the bargain-priced heavy wooden furniture no one else wanted from charity shops and printed out and pinned to the bedroom walls the twenty-two-page outline of this book, ready to get to work.

Peter lay in our recently assembled bed and looked dubiously at the neat grid of paper that documented every hard, painful thing I had ever lived through. 'Are you sure this is going to be OK?'

'It has to be.'

'It's not going to be upsetting?'

I shrugged. 'I've a book to write.'

But I didn't write the book. When you have grown up in a house where family loyalty comes second only to family secrecy, the act of saying aloud what has happened to you – even to people you love – is hard enough. The concept of writing those same words in a book that will be put into strangers' hands, hearts and potentially judgemental heads, is like learning to use your left hand instead of your right (in a situation that involves sawing off your right hand with the edge of a rusty Yale key).

I found a therapist, negotiating fortnightly appointments because that was what I could afford (and even then, at £100 a month, it felt like a wild luxury – our moderately stained sofa had only cost £50). I visited her at the top of an old, overly hot building in the Georgian Quarter that smelled of school dinners.

She was a gentle woman, fond of porridge-coloured jumpers, who always seemed so sad during our sessions that I wanted to invite her for a coffee afterwards and see how she was doing. When I told her of my difficulty in writing she said that her clients often felt, if they had grown up being told not to utter a word about what was happening in their childhood or had been constantly denied and belittled when they did, that their bodies seized up, their mouths refused to form words. Yes, I agreed, when I sit down to write it feels like an actual physical force is stopping me.

Around this time, I went down to London for the first *Lowborn* meetings. I went with my publisher's PR person to the *Pool* magazine's office where we discussed the book and what I might be able to write for them in the run-up to publication.

I had dreamed of writing for that particular magazine for quite some time. It was cool, feminist and people I admired wrote for it. Somehow it embodied a sort of acceptance, an arrival.

I raised my chin, spoke directly. 'This book's really about –' I was sure I could feel my heartbeat in the soles of my feet – 'if you're born poor you're fucked. But if you're born poor *and* a woman then you're genuinely and utterly fucked.'

After a twenty-minute meeting I left with the agreement I'd write them a column about poverty in the UK every month for a full year.

The next day I stood in the shining towers of Penguin Random House and handed round hipster sourdough doughnuts to the publishing team and then went for a Thai lunch with my agent and editor.

I'd spent two days smiling and hugging and making strange sort of celebratory exclamations with lots of people. It was real then, this book that had just been an intention and an idea. I'd kept up my persona beautifully. On the outside I was a woman who'd just had two career breakthroughs – my first non-fiction book deal and my first column – in an incredibly elitist industry, who was engaged to a man who she loved deeply, who'd just returned from living overseas for a year. On the outside I thought perhaps I looked exactly like them.

But after my last meeting was over I stood gripping the black railings of a private communal garden in Pimlico and wept. I wept because I now knew for certain that the writing of this book would be a process of turning myself inside out. That it would mean I could never again adopt my charming way, wear some decent clothes and 'pass'. I wept because I didn't know how to free myself from the tyranny of silence and the gnawing shame that came with that voicelessness, because I was terrified of writing this book and also terrified I'd have to live in this pretend sort of way forever if I didn't.

'Are you all right?' A young policewoman stepped towards me. 'Do you want me to call somebody?'

I straightened, smiled my polite smile, used the posh voice I'd used in those meetings. 'Thank you. That's kind. Just a bad day is all. I'm calling my partner now.'

'You're sure?'

I smiled a bigger smile. 'I'm sure. Thank you, you're kind.'

I called Peter and cried on the phone to him for another two hours, the screen slick and sliding about my face, my breath unable to keep up with me as I wandered the streets. Afterwards, I went to meet a friend who had troubles of her own and drank five pints. After three I stopped crying.

By the time I got on the coach to go back to Liverpool I had no idea if I was going to write this book at all.

I'd intended to go back to my old towns and cities over the winter. I booked a series of complex train and coach connections. I researched the places I would visit by trawling Google Images for areas I might remember. I read council reports on life expectancy and teenage sexual health and newspaper articles about stabbings and closed factories.

I called Aberdeen Council, my voice reedy with nerves.

'Hello, I'm . . . I'm trying to get access to my child protection documents. I think I was in care sometime between 1982 and –'

'Hold the line.'

That happened several times. I had to repeat the words over and over. Ones I'd never even said to my closest friends.

I don't know why, of all the things I've felt ashamed of as an adult, having been in foster care is the one that felt most taboo to speak aloud. Perhaps because the news is filled with the bad things that happen to vulnerable children when they are given to strangers, perhaps because I was only three or four and all I have is snapshots of that time, like those deeply hued vintage photographs where the red is especially red. Or maybe it's because I have spent so much of my time excusing the hurt and chaos of my childhood but something like being taken from your parent forcibly by law is incontrovertible proof. And because there's a particular sort of family where children are taken away from their mothers and I didn't want to think that my family, for all its complexities, was one of *those* families. Hunting the documents out, voicing the words even, was like waving a sign saying that was us. It was declaring war on those who were inclined to say that everything was fine, that I'd nothing to complain about. Even when that person was sometimes me.

I could feel the panic thrumming through my body as I finally spoke to the woman with the soft Aberdonian accent that sounded like home, also called Kerry, in Complaints and Enquiries, and she explained the process which involved a form and a payment of £10. I put down the phone and went shakily from my desk at the window, to the bed, got under the duvet and slept for an hour.

It wasn't her fault, that other Kerry, with a life that was probably so different from mine. I emailed to clarify a detail. When there was no response I sent a further email explaining I was writing a book that would be *published by Penguin Random House*, that I was a *journalist*. It's amazing how those words, indications of status, signifiers of a small sort of power, get wheels oiled. They waived the payment and my documents would be retrieved from among the forgotten others, all those kids, all those families who found themselves breaking either temporarily or for good.

Sitting at my desk in front of the tall windows I looked out at the busy road of shops and takeaways.

I was Skyping two STV producers who sat in a small room in a studio somewhere in Scotland. I could just make out their pixelated faces, nodding earnestly, just as I had nodded when they'd explained they were looking for people who'd experienced hidden homelessness to appear in a documentary as part of the station's annual fundraising appeal.

'And how was it, growing up that way?' they asked me.

I smiled. I've always smiled whenever discomfit, something too painful to confront, has risen up. I wore a great, shit-eating grin while writing a lot of this book.

I know, of course, that they were hoping I'd bare my throat.

They weren't being exploitative. I understood they were trying to build a story, just as I am doing here. So, I didn't blame them for hoping for drama, tears and tales of woe. Certainly, my calm, smiling face must have been a disappointment.

'You know, when you're a kid and that's your world, you don't realise how bad it is.' I gave a low laugh, another giveaway that I'm navigating the very edges of what I find tolerable.

'And what would you say life is like now? After growing up like that?'

I smiled wider. 'Well, I have a better life than I ever could have imagined. I have been hugely, hugely lucky.'

Neither statement is entirely true.

It's true that growing up in poverty and dysfunction, living from one week to another, knowing that nothing is stable, anything might be taken in a moment, and thinking of the future in ways that you know are either fantastical (I'll get discovered and make a Hollywood film!) or hopeless (who cares if I finish school anyway), was all I knew. That past, that psychology, is my foundation; it made me this woman.

But it's not true that I didn't know that things were bad, that I didn't recognise that we weren't like the families on TV, or like the many kids in my schools whose mums never wanted me playing with their children. I knew we were poor, really perilously poor, from the earliest age.

There was a game I used to play when I was around five or six. I'd lie on my bed in the crappy bed and breakfast we lived in, while Mum took one of her long afternoon sleeps, and I'd imagine that everything was the opposite – that the camp bed in the corner of the room that constituted our home was a four-poster bed draped with pink satin. That instead of my three second-hand cuddly toys with their stains from previous owners and a few tatty kids' books, I had an overflowing toy box. That the tight, pale face Mum had when she looked at the food on our shelf in the shared kitchen towards the end of the week would disappear because we were actually rich and could afford anything at all we wanted. Along with the hyper-vigilance a child will learn when constantly in foreign environments with strange people, my imagination was trained and fed by the way I grew up.

But yes, I am lucky too. My life now is a good one. Every day I marvel that I have purposeful work that I'm good at, a person who loves me who I have a healthy relationship with. A little rented flat we can afford and a fridge full of food.

And it was luck that brought me this life of simple, warm, stable pleasures.

There is nothing that is special about me. I am smart, I learn quickly and adapt well. I have a good imagination and found a way to express it. I know how to read situations and people. But no more so, and often a lot less, than many of the kids I grew up with.

So, if not pure, dumb, arbitrary luck then why is it me and not Elaine from the flat upstairs or Sam from two streets up writing this book?

Simply, the road rose up to meet me and fell from beneath the feet of the people who I played kiss chase with, who I practised the splits and *Dirty Dancing* routines with in the playground, who I broke into disused buildings and drank cider with on remote bridges and, eventually, who I staggered from club to club with, our skirts barely cradling the round of our little arses as we counted off the double figures of men we'd 'got off' with that night.

When I'm doing the PR rounds of newspaper and radio interviews, or at live events, in green rooms at literary festivals, or at parties where I'm always so grateful for the free bar, drinking two glasses of wine as quickly as possible from nerves, occasionally someone I'm speaking to will look at me appraisingly and say, 'You'd never guess, you know. How you grew up.'

I know it's meant to be a compliment. They look at my nice white teeth, only a little crooked, my body kept on the right side of plump by the exercise I do to quell the anxiety I still carry in my marrow. They look at my clothes that are mostly second-hand but carefully chosen, my big smile and loud, easy laugh I learned so that I might navigate this world. They look me over. And they give me a pass.

What they're actually saying is, 'You're not like them, you really do seem to be one of us.' And perhaps I have laughed, touched them on the arm and replied in a low voice, 'Wait until you see me after my fourth drink' or 'Oh, there's plenty of fishwife in me still, I promise.' And then I'll ask them a question and move the conversation along somewhere safer.

Because how can I say that what they are looking at is barely a real thing at all? That what they think is an achievement is just a layer that can be easily peeled away?

Why would I try to explain to them that while it is necessary to 'pass', the bones, blood and muscle, the very substance of me, belong to how I was raised? To those earliest years in those damp, chaotic flats?

The words I heard spoken to me in my first twenty years are tattooed everywhere under my skin. And they are just as alive and true as anything I've heard at those parties or festivals.

How could I say to that well-intentioned person, smiling at me benevolently, that I still carry that child with me? That often she seems impossibly heavy but sometimes it also feels that the child might, in fact, be carrying me and what they see and approve of is simply a costume of grown-up clothes I stand wearing in front of them?

5
Aberdeen
2017

My first research trip to Aberdeen was approaching. I'd tried to get in touch with my Uncle Mark, suggesting it would be nice to see him when I was up. I gave him my dates but never heard back. It was a relief to have that pressure taken off.

And then what was supposed to be my first trip home became, instead, my agreeing to shoot that short segment on hidden home-lessness for the STV Appeal with the producers I'd Skyped with. Which took the pressure off even further. But the morning I was due to leave, anxiety flooded back over me again. Peter, who had been working in the other room, came through and found me at the computer with thirty minutes to spare looking at a train-booking website.

'Sweetheart, you'll be late.'

'I know, I know it's just . . . I wish you were coming with me. I'd feel so much better if you were there.'

Thirty minutes later, for the price of almost half our monthly rent, we had a last-minute ticket for Peter and we were on the train together, me hugging his unshowered body, his hastily packed bag full of dirty laundry.

If I sound like a child here, it's because that's how I felt. Like a child fearful of something under the bed even after the bed has been checked and the doors have been locked, the light left on. I hadn't been back to Aberdeen in twenty-four years and I had come to believe that if I stepped a foot there somehow the spell I had woven, the life I had created for myself, would simply crumble away and it would be like I'd never left at all. Just like a child's fear, it was wholly irrational but felt completely real.

If it sounds like Peter is the best partner I could wish for it's because he is. I had never been so fully and so consistently loved. I had never been in a relationship where I was allowed to be sad or angry. Where I didn't fear that in being my flawed, fractured self I would break what we had, and in which vulnerability wasn't punished.

Peter simply stayed by my side and loved me and that seemed like a form of magic. I wanted him to be on my first step of that journey because I hoped that magic would be enough to protect me.

When I thought of Aberdeen I thought of hard, grey granite buildings rising up, looming even, into an even greyer sky. I thought about dark, cracked pavements, shiny from the freezing rain, tumbling with crisp bags and broken glass sparkling in gutters. If you asked me to remember something happy then I'd tell you about eating smoked kippers, 'smokies', with my mum straight from the paper bag, of a warm bus in winter or blustery walks to the Bay of Nigg (we'd pronounce it buy-a-nigg) where the blonde fluff of my hair rose up all around me and I felt like I could be swept away and fly. I only have one memory of sunshine, as if summers didn't exist in Aberdeen: me, Mum, Jimmy in the garden, overgrown nettles and empty cans on a spread-out blanket. But in the end, that was no sunny-day memory at all.

I knew the city would have changed. Now when I said I was from Aberdeen people would say, 'Posh!' or, 'Your family must have been well off,' or, most bewilderingly to me, 'Oh, lovely!' I knew black gold had washed itself over our hard and unforgiving city, making it shiny if not brand new. I knew it was now considered expensive, chichi even. It had golf courses and four-star hotels. But still, I thought I'd know it somehow.

When we arrived we exited the train station through a big glass shopping centre. Walking past Carluccio's, Starbucks and YO! Sushi, everything and everyone looked rich. Rich in the way that me and Mum used to say it to mean, 'They can afford to spend twenty quid without thinking about it. They can go out for dinner just because they fancy it. Or buy a bottle of wine. They won't even know how much they have in their purse.' Which all made sense, given in 2018 Aberdeen moved up twelve places to become the 134th most costly place to live in the world on the Mercer Cost of Living Survey.

I can only describe the sensation of walking through that shopping centre, past Hugo Boss and Michael Kors, as the disorientating feeling of visiting a futuristic film set of your life – there's no doubt it's the right place but everything seems wrong too.

But it wasn't just me. Things *were* going badly wrong in my old home town. Despite it being so expensive, for years the city had been facing serious economic decline. The price of oil had slumped and Aberdeen's very foundations had been built first on fish and then on oil. Without those to keep it afloat, it was sinking.

Initially, it was hard for me to feel much sympathy when I heard of oil executives driving their Porsches to foodbanks, but then I realised what that really meant. It meant taxi drivers with no fares and waitresses with no shifts. It meant fewer jobs all round. Unemployment figures in Scotland's third largest city had increased by 25% since 2015, when oil prices per barrel dropped from $120 to around $30. This in turn had meant record use of foodbanks in Aberdeen, with Community Food Initiatives North East (CFINE) distributing approximately 1.1 million meals – 71,000 food parcels – in 2017. It hardly broke my heart when I heard Trump's golf course was failing because no one could afford to play on it any more. Then I remembered that when the rich slide that continues down to poor folk, who've already been living on just enough to get by and their wits. And when that happens, there's nowhere to slide but off the very edge.

Our accommodation for the night was an expensive businessmen's hotel by the station, the kind that is decorated in muted browns, beiges and maroons. After we checked in we stretched out on the cool, crisp cotton sheets. Peter kissed my temple.

'How are you doing?' I shook my head. Said nothing. 'Just think, would you have ever thought when you left that when you finally came back you'd be staying in a fancy hotel and meeting a TV team the next day who want to interview you because you write novels?'

No, I hadn't. And I wasn't sure I liked it. Where, I wondered, was my Aberdeen? I'd thought, no matter how reluctantly, I was coming home.

Perhaps if I'd gone straight to Torry, the part of town where my family had lived for decades, I wouldn't have had that initial strange, dislocated feeling. The data collected from all of Scotland's 6,976 'data zones' puts Torry in the top 7% of the most deprived, particularly in essential areas such as employment, education and housing. Which is particularly shocking in the light of Aberdeen's ranking in the Mercer survey. There was clearly a lot of the old Aberdeen left. We just hadn't found it yet.

The next morning, I put on my smart 'TV clothes' and met the producer and cameraman. We walked through Aberdeen towards the bookshop where I'd be filmed for the initial interview. I still didn't recognise anything.

I sometimes do the occasional interview on film when I'm promoting books, but this was my first time talking about my own life and also about something as potentially contentious as home-lessness. I'd researched, I had stats, I'd considered my position and the representation of my own experiences as a kid. I'd thought about how much I was willing to say, where my line was. The pro-ducer and cameraman were both warm and kind, they showed me pictures of their partners and kids. The producer told me about her dachshund puppy, love of bum bags and Celine Dion. Still, under the lights, I was nervous.

After the interview, the producer said, 'You talk just like a politician,' and I said, 'Thank you,' though I've no doubt it wasn't a compliment.

Next, we were to drive to my first flat. I remember that flat so vividly in my mind though we left it when I was around three. I am often frustrated by my memory. Why can I remember precisely how sunburn peeled in sheets from my shins or the way those glossy plastic fruits spilled out sherbet? Why can I remember the dance I did to Kylie in the playground and the little 'Secret Keep-ers' toys shaped like snail princesses and Push Pops (Don't push me, push a Push Pop!) that I so longed for? Why those things and not the order of where we lived, the journeys between them, the schools I attended and left?

Probably because it was these things that made up the fabric of my childhood life. What I cared about was chocolate biscuits, *Danger Mouse* and then Timmy Mallett, Bros, birthday parties and whether I would ever be able to stretch myself into the splits (spoiler: I couldn't).

The other explanation of these blank spots, which are like someone has taken a rubber to the paper of my consciousness, is that I simply blocked out stressful things. But that house, I remember.

Jimmy, I remember. That feeling of having no one caring for me, of danger and abandonment, I remember.

The producer had hired a car to drive us out to Manor Avenue on my old estate. They'd asked if I could give them my name for insurance, thinking I would drive, until I explained that I'd never learned when I was young and then I'd lived in London and what was the point? Just like I had to explain there were few to no photos of me as a child (no money for a camera, film or developing, so many moves where things were left behind). I sat in the back while they filmed me from the front seat, the mic pack digging into me.

'Just tell us how you're feeling.'

We drove out of the city, through the streets of the nicer, bigger houses with trimmed hedges and painted benches, up past a Shell garage towards streets and streets of the same blocky grey buildings, where everything just looked a bit less cared for, a little more broken.

'Oh, now I'm starting to recognise some things.'

I knew as soon as we turned the corner. I knew as soon as we were outside the house. I could have probably walked there from the Shell garage. That microphone was pointless. I was speechless.

A hulking granite building made up of four flats, it looked permanent but so basic it seemed not quite finished. Of course, it appeared smaller, though I hadn't expected it to. The front yard was still as scrubby as ever and littered with toys, and when I wandered to the back I saw a Wendy house, a few bikes strewn about.

I looked up to our window and all the memories flooded across my eyes, but that was all, I was only observing it from my taller, protected vantage point, just like the camera was observing me. Right then, I felt the years between being a scared kid and that moment as an adult as if they formed a safety barrier.

The footage shows me with my arms wrapped around myself and the wind whipping my hair. I stare up at my old window and look like I'm about to cry. Instead I smile the smallest smile.

While I was staring a big man, wearing overalls, with a fuzz of ginger hair and a scatter of freckles, parked up in a van. He reminded me of my Uncle Mark.

'What're you doin' with that filming?'

I smiled instinctively – I wanted him to know there was nothing to worry about. I reached out my hand and he looked at his and then took mine.

'Sorry. Is it OK? I used to live here. That one up there. When I was a baby. I haven't been back in thirty-four years.' I shook my head at him. 'It hasn't changed a bit, you know.'

I saw him relax then. The producer and the cameraman had moved down the street and it was just me and him and our house.

He nodded, tucked his hands in his overalls and then took them out again. He didn't look at me but up at the windows. 'I went back to my nan's house a few months ago.'

'It's strange, isn't it? How did you find it?'

'Aye, it was weird.' He looked at me, shy for such a big man, but smiling. 'Only thing I remembered was I got stung by a bee in her garden.' He gestured around him. 'They're all coming down in a coupla months.' We both stared at the house for a few more moments. 'Well, I'd best get in.'

'Thanks very much for letting me do this. I appreciate it.'

'Aye, aye.' He raised his hand and then walked inside my old home.

I did a little segment to the camera with the boarded-up houses already waiting for demolition behind me. I talked about all the things that make a home: warmth and comfort, furniture and pride in your surroundings, stability and community. I spoke about how hard it is to grow up on estates where you know no one gives a fuck about you or where you're living. I wondered how the kids who played in their Wendy house in my old backyard felt about seeing their neighbourhood boarded up and die around them. 'You want to feel you're growing up somewhere that's alive. Otherwise, what are you meant to assume about your own future?'

Just as we were getting back in the car a lanky guy came out of the house and approached us. He leaned in the window to speak to me.

'Hiya, I saw you filmin' my auntie's window up there.'

'Is it OK? It's just I lived there when I was a baby. It's the first time I've been back. I'm sorry if we disturbed you.'

'Naw, naw problem, it's just –' he smiled, leaned in further and lowered his voice – 'my auntie's got her washing up on the clothes dryer by the window and she's worrying. She was hoping you could blur out her knickers, like.'

We both howled with laughter and I promised her washing wouldn't end up on the telly. 'Fair play. I wouldn't like that either.'

I left my old home with him waving us goodbye and me still laughing my head off about his auntie's nearly famous knickers. It did, at least for a moment, seem a little like home.

I thought the trip had been a success. I went back to the hotel, sat on the edge of the bed chugging down a can of G&T, and told Peter that it had been strange and a little sad but I'd realised I was grown and it couldn't hurt me any more. That night we ate cheeseburgers for dinner and saw a terrible film.

But the next day I felt filleted by exhaustion. I was tearful and irritable and tender.

We returned to Liverpool and I went to bed for a few days. Still I didn't write.

A few weeks later the news about *Lowborn*, the book I wasn't writing yet, was announced in the *Bookseller* magazine. The day was spoked with excitement and adrenaline. Finally, my news was out and people I loved and respected were sending through messages of support and enthusiasm. Suddenly, in the face of all that encouragement and goodwill, it didn't seem so scary telling all my secrets, returning to all my dark places, looking at the communities who've been in the shit for decades and trying to not feel the weight of the futility in that.

I was galvanised by the idea that perhaps I could actually make a difference. That people might listen. That rather than doing something shameful, it might be something *good*. That there might not be some unseen, terrifying punishment for breaking ranks and silence. I took the kindness of friends, colleagues and strangers and used their voices to muffle the louder ones in my head.

But I woke the next morning at 4.20. And 4.20 a.m. is not my friend. As I lay in bed I felt my excitement grinding down to anxiety. Later that morning, Peter and I argued, I don't even remember what about, and the rest of the day was spent in strange, uneasy reconciliation as we moved around each other tentatively. I managed a shower and a change of pyjamas. I wrote three sentences of an email to a writer I was mentoring and then gave up.

That evening, still in the swirl of unease, I sought comfort in empty TV and toad-in-the-hole drenched in gravy. It was 11 p.m. when I heard the ping on my computer. I had been clicking between accounts replying to congratulatory messages with exclamation marks that were no longer honest.

The message was from my Uncle Mark, posted under a cheesy joke on my Facebook wall. It said:

Hi, it's Uncle Mark I was hoping you would have con-tacted me when you were up. I'm not daft the it reason u kept in touch with was for information for your STV Homeless crusade NOT A PEEP Dont you EVER try and use me again to make yourself look good whoever is reading this be careful of this girl she will use u to her own ends then drop you like a stone. I'm embarrassed to call you my niece.

It was posted on my public wall and though it featured his usual eccentric spelling and grammar the fact that they were better than usual made me think he wasn't, as I'd first thought, lashing out. It seemed designed to shame me. To turn people against me. It felt nasty and destructive and it was untrue. I deleted it immediately.

I called Peter over from his desk and he sat beside me, our knees tucked up together as we tried to work out with two comput-ers side by side, searching multiple forums, how I could stop him speaking to me that way again in public.

I replied in a private message to Uncle Mark. No, I said, I did not use you. The last message above is from me and it said when I'd be in town. Posting on my public wall seemed destructive and childish. It made me understand what sort of relationship I could hope for from him.

Then I blocked my uncle. With a click that connection to my family was gone once again.

And then I started writing.

6
Latvia
2017

I received the child protection documents three weeks before Christmas. On the day they arrived with Peter in Liverpool I had just started a three-week writing residency at the Writers' and Translators' House in Ventspils, Latvia.

Ventspils is a small port town a few hours from Riga and arriving there was very much like walking into a Christmas card. There was a twenty-foot fairy-light-strewn tree in the main square that the gingerbread house I would be staying in looked out on. Inside there was a large kitchen, a cosy library, gentle German and Russian translators in big jumpers and an ancient, lazy black cat called Rudi.

I was already nervous that day, even before Peter left a voice message saying the thick envelope, ticking like a bomb, had arrived at our flat. Almost all social situations scare me. My instinct is always to believe that I will not be liked. That my efforts, often excessive, to be warm and friendly and interested, will be rebuffed. I smile too much, am too enthusiastic, laugh too loudly and too quickly. I ask too many questions of people, perhaps deflecting any focus from myself because I am sure what there is of me doesn't stand up to scrutiny.

I called Peter back on a crackling line while walking through Ventspils to find a supermarket. I wore two coats and kept my head bowed against the horizontal sleet as I walked in circles around the town's near-identical streets full of wooden houses.

'Please, will you scan them and send them to me? I feel like

I've been waiting such a long time for this. And now I might have some . . . some clues.'

Clues. I'd been using that term a lot. As though this was somehow abstract, and I was a private investigator digging away at the mysteries of another person who used to exist. Which is in fact how it often felt.

'I will, Kerry. I just want you to be OK.' His voice sounded small, like a little boy's. I realised he was frightened for me.

'Honestly, Peter, it's OK. I need to know this stuff. Whatever it is. Maybe it will make some kind of sense of things. Prove I don't have night terrors or terrible anxiety or a fear of any sort of social situation for no reason.' I found myself back where I started, outside an undeniably Eastern European department store, the window full of dummies wearing beige anoraks. 'Even if I found out the worst thing I possibly could it wouldn't surprise me.'

'OK then. OK.' He sounded so sad. 'I love you so much.'

There were fifty-six pages in total. Grainy scans, sheaves of reports and letters, a long list of dates and actions. And across them all, thick black lines, 'redacted', hiding the real information. I'd only ever seen that in spy films and it instantly gave me the impression that the documents might have all the answers if I could simply decode them.

In my unfamiliar little room, I put on some music and made a cup of tea. I was in good spirits I told myself, I was grown now and far away. Look at me, in Latvia! I waited impatiently while the scans downloaded, like someone ripping open a present from an enemy, or perhaps their lover's diary. Eager, guilty, sure nothing good will be inside.

The first few pages were about the initial referral from the head of my nursery school in Aberdeen, where my mum had turned up 'drunk and not in a fit state to care for the child'. Arrangements were made for me under a 'place of safety' record and I was taken into emergency foster care. It was September 1983 and I was almost three years old. The term, 'place of safety', unhooked something inside of me, exposed a raw part. There was never any safety.

The next file was my nursery application from a few months earlier. It contained a reference to a 'closed case'. I looked into it later and found out my mum had asked for a nursery place when I was one. She was in arrears with her rent and utilities. The request was refused since I wasn't able to go into nursery until I was two. They advised Mum to go to the DSS.

Next there were official forms. A document proposing to remove me from my mum's care. My mum's curlicue signature, the same pretty signature I learned to copy in my teens, so much like a teenage girl's.

Over the years I was told many versions of the story of how I ended up in care. Many featured interfering 'do-gooder' social workers; others revolved around me being given away on a whim and my mum moving heaven and earth to get me back like the hero of a disaster film. None of them involved Mum turning up drunk to nursery or offering minimal cooperation.

There were five further letters. Three trying to arrange appointments with my mum and expressing regret that my mum was out during the scheduled visit; another requesting expenses, for a fireguard and clothes, for my foster-parent. The final one from the social worker saying my mum must be glad to have me back but she was there if there were any difficulties in the future. In that letter I detected no small note of defeat. A white flag written across a page in typewriter ink.

The first report in the next file was dated 5 October, around three weeks after I was put into care. These were the first of the documents with large sections blacked out, like they belonged in a totalitarian regime. The first document detailed how on my mum's second visit to see me, she immediately left me with <names redacted> and it later came to light that she had been run over by an articulated lorry and taken to casualty. 'The police indicated that she was extremely lucky.'

The entire paragraph explaining what had happened was just one solid black block. It went on to say that my mum was trying to pressurise my grandma into taking me. The reason the social worker didn't feel Grandma was fit enough to take care of me was stolen from me by a thick black line. There was a line about my mum setting up house with her boyfriend – I assume that was Jimmy, the one with the nunchucks. The report stated that since my birth my mum had gone from 'crisis to crisis . . . resulting in the involvement of a number of family members and agencies'. The report described Mum as 'immature' and 'impulsive' and suggested another twenty-one days in foster care before further review. On my third birthday the social worker dropped me off at my grandma's where there was a little party for me. The note said my mum had 'made a great fuss' buying me 'presents, balloons and a birthday cake'.

I was returned home, against the social worker's recommendation, at the end of October.

The following report was from 1 December, two and a half months after I had been returned home from foster care. It said my mum refused to cooperate with the social workers, that following a row with nursery staff where they queried her work and who was picking me up, my mum withdrew me from nursery.

Then there was a report from February. It described the social worker's frustrations at my mum's lack of commitment to changing, evidenced by the number of broken appointments. She said that there was still cause for concern about my home life and my well-being and there were likely to be more difficulties but 'until a further referral is made there is nothing more that can be done'.

I do not understand this. I understand there are many children who go through worse than I ever did but I also understand that someone, anyone, should have been protecting me. I was three years old.

The next report had two large paragraphs blacked out. Big black holes on the page. Looking at them made me feel like I was holding my breath. It was frustrating to be so close to what I considered to be the truth and be denied it. What right did they have to tell me what I should or should not know? I went to Google and searched for ways to take back those sentences, scrub away the black, so that I would have all the dots in place to join for myself. But it's impossible. I continued to read.

Another report outlined my mum's situation prior to turning up drunk at nursery that day – no job, left me a lot with 'childminders', struggled to cope. It described me as a 'bright and attractive' young girl. When Peter read the reports later he told me it was proof that I was always 'radiant, an anomaly given your situation', but my interpretation is perhaps more telling: that attractive little girls shouldn't be left without protection, that they shouldn't be left with strangers, who knows what will happen. It said the nursery staff felt I settled in 'almost too easily' and that I 'showed no signs of being unhappy or upset' at being away from home. It said how these 'observations were concerning'.

There was a summary of me: 'Happy, cheerful'. 'Small but active'. 'Talks a lot but rather indistinctly'. 'Rather isolated'. In my room in Latvia with the rain lashing I laughed at how this could be used to describe me now too. The notes frequently referred to my mother's 'ambivalence' about keeping me. It said I was a poor eater, a poor walker, that I enjoyed nursery when I could attend. It said that after I was removed from her care, I 'hadn't asked anymore' for my mother 'at all'. Like a bell ringing somewhere, reading that made me feel guilty and disloyal.

During the course of writing this book I acquired pictures of the party the social worker had taken me to while in care. The photos have my mum's handwriting on the back, 'Kerry's 3rd birthday'. In one my mum, beautiful and big-eyed, stands behind me as I blow out my candles. In another Mum and Grandma lean into each other, felled by booze, me in the middle with a dirty face, my grandma wearing a skewed child's cowboy hat, her skirt rising up and showing her slip. I wondered, given that only a week previously Mum had almost been killed by the truck, given that Grandma had refused to take me in, given that I was only there for a few hours before being returned to a stranger, how this joy could have been so easily reached. I tried to detect a note of regret or even hysteria in the pictures but I saw nothing but two drunk women and a kid full of cake.

I'd last seen that picture when I'd gone to see my mother in my mid-twenties. I was in a stable relationship and trying to make sense of my world. I told my mum I was having counselling to deal with the difficulties of my childhood. She flew into a rage. Her rages always begin with a silence, a few deep breaths, as though gathering steam, and then the anger. Pure, unadulterated rage. Her small, slim body tight, her fists balled. And though you know you are bigger than her, and likely stronger, you will quake. And, as you have learned to do, you will shut off, tell her you're leaving. You'll begin to gather your things, crying, shouting back, she will follow you screaming at you in the small, hot living room.

She'll disappear for a minute, no more, and you'll move

quickly, hands shaking as you check you have what you need, purse, keys, phone, stuffing things into your bag, crying and dizzy.

That particular visit, when she appeared again she had a battered navy-blue leather clutch that she once used for her brother's wedding but which now held photos. She took them out screaming, 'You weren't happy? You say you weren't happy? What's this?' She pulled photos out and shoved them at me, and then she crumpled the birthday photo and threw it in my face.

I pushed her away, just a few more things to gather and then I could run. Truly, for someone barely five foot she was terrifying.

I wept and my heart thundered as she screamed, 'What's this then? And this? And this?' And she chased me round the house, grabbing those pictures of me as a child, my smiling face, looking so happy, and ripping them up before throwing the pieces in my face.

As I left I told her I was never coming back. This was not OK. And she screamed that I was no daughter of hers.

But it was only when I read the documents that I realised the happy childhood she had ripped up in my face was actually one of being shunted from place to place, of chaos and instability, and painting on a smile whatever was happening.

The next child protection document described how, at a home visit around four months after I'd returned home from foster care, the social worker arrived to find workmen renovating the flat and Mum living in a single room. There was a party going on. Mum was 'verbally aggressive' and asked the social worker to leave.

Because she hadn't seen me and she wanted to know who had care of me, the social worker visited later in the day and my mum was gone. Then the police came and checked Mum was there. She was, but I was not. She told them I was with her cousin. After this, things become a bit harder to follow. It seems I was left with my mum's cousin Craig. But he had taken me somewhere else – <names redacted> – perhaps some kind of boarding house. Then I went to another foster home for four days until a child hearing. Despite the social worker's concerns I was returned to Mum.

The social worker interviewed my grandma, aunt, one of Mum's cousins and two mystery childminders and all of them voiced concerns but Mum would not cooperate. When the social worker came to do a house visit Mum was 'so aggressive' she made me cry.

Document 25 simply said 'CORRESPONDENCE'. It began with a letter from July 1984. 'Investigated the case further by interviewing various family members. Although much concern was expressed regarding the care of Kerry by her mother, there was little presented in the way of concrete evidence.'

And I wondered again, how could they have left me there? And what sort of evidence was required beyond our family members saying that it wasn't good to leave me with Mum? It went on: 'It is also important to acknowledge that although Miss Mackie agreed to cooperate . . . her levels of cooperation were minimal.'

Almost a year after my first referral, on 21 August 1984, the case was closed. Nothing could be done until a 'further referral was made'.

Sitting there at my desk in the nice residency I was paid to attend by the British Council, I was at a seemingly comfortable time in both my life and career. As someone who I hope will always try and comprehend why rather than simply assume the worst, I wanted to give everyone involved a modicum of compassion. I wanted to try and understand the motivations and hardships involved in such a complex situation.

But then there was that child. And I realised my childhood made itself known to me every single day. In the way I engaged with others, when I slept, when and what I ate. In the thought patterns seemingly designed to undermine me, to make me feel beneath whoever I was interacting with, which made me beg in all sorts of ways for their approval. In the deep loneliness, the way I often said I was a 'black hole for love', no matter how much I had been and was loved in my adult life.

I thought of the fear which pumped every second beat of my heart. Always, always there, like a sharp whistle of tinnitus. Suddenly, I could see the connections clearly. I could pluck at the strings linking 'now' to 'then'. But it also seemed, despite years of trying, I had no power to sever or change them. And then I felt angry at everyone.

Sitting in that little room far from home, in that cosy, lonely house filled with strangers, I cried and raged in the way a child will seem to for no reason. I tried to do it quietly so that the others would not hear me and, eventually, I called Peter and spoke to him in sprawling monologues about everything I'd read. He told me how sad it made him. How he couldn't imagine it. How glad he was that I was me now, whatever had made me that way.

At one point I told him, furious, 'If I had a little child, I would never let it out of my sight with a stranger for even an hour. I'd love it so well.' At the other end of the phone he was silent and then eventually he said, 'I know, I know you would. I'm sorry. I love you.'

That night, unable to sleep, I remembered how Mum used to say to me, as the ultimate threat, 'You think this is bad? I'll put you into care.'

I heard many variations of this hollow threat throughout my childhood and teens. Except I knew it wasn't hollow. Even if I couldn't remember the details I knew I had been taken into care before. I was all too aware how fragile and collapsible my world was.

Once, aged around seven or eight, I called her bluff and packed a bag for me and my baby sister and went to bed that night fully expecting we'd be taken into care the next morning 'once the office was open'. But it was all forgotten as soon as we sat down with our cereal in front of the TV.

In my teens, I must have been about fifteen, we actually got as far as the social welfare office in Great Yarmouth. Mum said she was done with me and I didn't want to live in her house any more either. She made it sound quite appealing – 'They'll put you up until you're sixteen and then you'll get your own benefits.'

The office's receptionist – God knows what she'd seen coming through those doors in her time – gave Mum a steely look and asked if she was sure about this. Mum said nothing, I shrugged and, somehow, we found ourselves outside on the pavement again, walking through town side by side, faces tight with misery, back to the house. I remember the scorched taste of averted disaster in my mouth.

In bed in Latvia, I imagined looking after that child who was me. How I would make it breakfast and encourage it to eat and listen as it talked on and on in the way children do, adoringly seeking out the adult who'll protect them, who'll show them how to live in this world. I would take that child on my lap and lean my chin on top of her soft blonde head of hair and she would know she was safe and loved and wanted.

After a week that burning feeling of rejection subsided. I truly understood that it really was no one's fault. That life is too messy to attribute blame so neatly. How can you blame ill and dysfunctional people living in an ill and dysfunctional society? How could

I blame my mum when she was simply struggling herself? How could I blame my father when the stories I knew of his childhood pointed to terrible abandonment and abuse? Or blame my grandmother for just trying to live her life as well as she could though it was full of struggles?

There was no culpability. Only fragments to be picked up, examined, partly understood and pieced together to tell this story. There were no answers in those records. Only that life was sometimes brutal to those who were vulnerable and without options.

But the blame didn't really go away, it shifted. The more I thought about my experiences in care, the angrier I became. It seemed to me that from the moment a child is born, the very moment it comes out scratching and covered in shit and blood and the pulverised insides of its mother, if that child is born on the margins, if the mother is defenceless and poor, then the struggle begins as soon as the first air burns into its tiny lungs.

That child, and other children from the most deprived 10% of neighbourhoods, is 18.5 times more likely than those in the least deprived to be on the child protection register. That kids like me, from the poorest parts of Scotland, are 20 times more likely to end up in care than those in the most affluent areas. And still there is no policy that takes into account poverty and social work interventions together. I suppose that those children will be poor is seen as a given but not as a cause, not as an overwhelming contributing factor that should be tackled.

What I experienced, even before the age of four, are the symptoms of a society that is structurally and systematically designed to further marginalise those who are struggling and those who are poor. These stories need to be told because society wishes to look in the other direction, because we do not want to think of the children a few streets away who have eaten shit food and not nearly enough of it, in a house where the heat isn't on and they don't own a single book, in threadbare clothes that are too small for them, being cared for by a parent who desperately requires help themselves.

Perhaps it's easier, though, not to acknowledge cause and effect, because if we did look at what was really happening, surely we wouldn't be able to live with that?

7
Aberdeen
1983

After that terrible year of foster homes and missed appointments and 'disruptions', it seems that for a while things got better for me and Mum. We got moved out of Manor Avenue to a proper estate in Torry, near Grandma and Mum's aunties and cousins. Our flat was in a small block and it made me feel safe to be surrounded by people. I got a spacehopper and spent hours bouncing up and down our landing. There was an ice-cream van and sometimes I'd have 10p or 20p grasped in my palm as I ran downstairs as fast as I could, jumping three steps at a time, my heart pummelling with elation and fear that he might go before I got to the van's window to buy jawbreakers.

My Uncle Mark made good money on the rigs and bought me a rocking horse with a proper hair mane and thick soft brown fur. I made friends with a girl my age and her younger brother and my mum made friends with their parents. We'd run around the estate together from morning until dusk then we'd go back to their two-storey flat, which in London might have been called something fancy like a duplex but in Aberdeen was just their council flat. We'd jump between the mattresses upstairs, while my mum and the grown-ups drank cheap booze downstairs. We were always given eggs and frozen chips at their place. Which was another reason I liked it there so much.

For a while it was just like being a kid.

In our new flat, I had my own room, but I liked the living room best, especially the spot on the carpet so near the electric fire my skin would blotch and the thick orange curtains that I'd spin and spin myself in until they swallowed my hair up, pulled my face tight. We had a sound system with a dead spider in the radio panel, frozen stiff-legged, who I called my friend.

We sometimes went to the sea at the Bay of Nigg and one day we found a kitten under one of the caravans there. Mum said the 'gypsies' wouldn't mind so we took it home. It had no meow, only an anguished squeal, so I named it Squeak. There was golden sunshine in that flat in the summer and, in the winter, though the windowpanes would freeze over, all the bars of the fire glowed bright. I had vitamin drops that smelled like banana to go in my daily glass of milk. I learned to butter toast. We watched *Dallas* or *Wogan* with our dinner on our laps.

But slowly things started to unravel again. I would wake up hours before Mum every morning and cause mischief. I emptied the plastic bag where she kept all her letters and receipts and photos and sat on top of them, unfolding and examining every single item as *Sesame Street* played in the background. I cut my own fringe with a pair of frog scissors.

Mum slept later and later. Sometimes she thought my antics were hilarious and sometimes she'd 'blow'. I always started out believing it would be the former but as the hours passed and she still hadn't woken, a black snake of anxiety would coil inside my stomach. When she did finally come downstairs I'd already be crying and begging for her not to be upset.

After a few months, perhaps even less, Mum decided we were leaving Aberdeen. We boarded a National Express with what we could carry – which wasn't much at all. I cried for my rocking horse and my kitten who we put back under the caravan where we'd found him. We departed in a hurry, with no money except that week's benefits and nowhere to go.

Maybe Mum needed 'a change'. Maybe we left because she was sick of the social services, 'fucking busybodies', always being able to 'interfere' when they wanted to. Or because she was angry with my family about my going into care in the first place, believing they should have rallied around and stopped it. Maybe it really was for the fabled 'fresh start' that we chased intermittently until I was fifteen.

But I think it was probably because she wanted to give me to my dad.

8
Liverpool
2018

When January came around I felt less and less inclined to go 'home' to my old towns. It seemed this strange process was splitting me in half. I was an archivist of my dead life. I was a private investigator digging my way through my own deeply buried secrets, both desperate for answers and fighting to keep them hidden.

I spoke at a British Council conference in Berlin. It was a rare glitzy event, well paid, with a four-star hotel, a thick envelope of cash for 'expenses', taxis to boozy meals at nice restaurants every night and a glossy brochure with the guest writers' faces, including mine, in it.

Everyone was friendly. I admired the other writers. But there was something in the experience that repelled me. I read from *Lowborn* on the first night and felt so raw, so exposed, for the remaining days. I drank more than I should have and couldn't sleep for the sound of trams on the street below and my own circular thoughts. I was due my period and my belly was so swollen, it felt as though a sharp word might pierce and shatter me. I spent the rest of the conference giving newspaper interviews and talking on panels about sex and gender with a thin smile and courteousness ineffectually cloaking my shocking, inexplicable hurt and anger.

I came home tender, tearful and confused. After all, wasn't this the life? Wasn't it wonderful to get to stand on a stage and have people listen? What did I have to complain about? 'I can't go on those research trips,' I told Peter, 'I can't.'

I rearranged the train tickets for a month away. Then, as if I'd wished it so, fell ill with a virus when it was time to go. I listened to the train helpline tell me I couldn't make any more changes to my tickets with a sort of gruff paternalism. The call centre was based in India and I imagined they thought it was horrifically wasteful, which, in fact, it was. With no painkillers in the house I'd resorted to sticking an entire clove of garlic in my ear and whimpered down the phone, 'I know. But I'm sick and there's nothing I can do.' And there was a frustrated sigh at the other end, as if we all knew the truth was that I was avoiding things that couldn't be avoided. 'Can I assist you with anything else?'

'You can reassure me I'm not grieving for my childhood. That my heart isn't breaking for the little girl who still walks with me every single day. That I'm not entirely stuck in all sorts of ways,' is what I might have said.

But I just said no thank you and laid my head back down on my garlic-scented pillow.

Perhaps it goes without saying that I was nervous. And just getting over a nasty virus that still pinched at my lungs and clogged my ears. I'd been careful to only take a chalky nibble of the travel sickness pill on the coach but still there was a drowsiness that weighed heavily. To this, in Golders Green Starbucks, while Peter proofread an article I needed to file and I tried to pin my hair up so I might look more respectable, I added three beta blockers, designed to cap adrenaline, still shaking hands, slow the pounding heart.

It was during one of my early-morning writing sessions that I had decided to contact my Aunt Alison. It was a new habit, waking at 6.30 a.m., making a cup of black coffee, writing at my desk by the window in the velvet hush, cold seeping through the glass, with the pale Liverpool light slowly turning the indigo dark to daytime, the wild garden swaying in conversation with the winter wind. Those mornings made me feel in control of this unwieldy process for the first time. The world of childhood, because I wasn't quite awake, came fluidly. After writing I'd sit at my desk until Peter woke – caffeinated and bouncing around the Internet: a *Guardian* article, a podcast, wedding dresses, arts cinemas, friends' Facebook updates, yoga videos, biscuit recipes, Twitter, a running playlist, running training plans, charity projects, plane tickets to places I wouldn't travel to.

I'd looked before of course. Once my Uncle Mark had been in touch I'd gone through his contacts on Facebook with the thoroughness of a private investigator, and when I'd found my mum, I'd found my aunt. I'd tried to remember what I'd been told about her. I couldn't really recall her myself. Mum had spoken about her with a combination of jealousy and reverence. She held her up as an example and a cautionary tale. She was rich. She came home from work and made clothes on her sewing machine for her two kids, 'Hannah and Liam', always to be spoken of jointly as though they were conjoined. She lived in Somerset, a place that had once sounded exotic. She had the singing voice of an angel. She knew what she wanted. She went after it and left everyone behind. She'd forgotten about them. I knew that she'd joined the navy (though I'll find out later she was actually a helicopter mechanic). That she was the 'good daughter'. I knew I hadn't seen her in twenty-six years.

That particular morning, I looked again at her Facebook. A post about Remembrance Sunday. A picture of her browsing pottery in a floral scarf. A picture of her with her daughter, pink light-up bras over sports kit, about to do a charity event. I searched my grown-up cousin's face for the wee girl I used to play with but I couldn't see it. They looked happy though, arms around each other, laughing. Next, there was a picture of her with her son, both holding medals after a race.

It was impulse. She was the last untested link. I opened messenger.

So we were off to meet my aunt and uncle-in-law, travelling down from Liverpool and across London to a little cafe I had suggested by Hammersmith Tube, a hipster Australian place called Truth (unintentionally foreboding, I just went with what was suggested by folks on Twitter), which probably wasn't to their taste at all.

They were already there with their coffee cups emptied in front of them. She wore a purple fleece, a shiny metallic poppy pin. Bobby, her husband of forty-odd years, sat beside her in a check shirt, V-neck sweater. They looked, well, just so normal. They looked like geography teachers on a trip to London.

We hugged warmly and I adopted my own usual cheerful, schoolteacher-ish manner. She looked like someone who had laughed a lot in her life. Her hand gestures were slightly jerky, she talked fast and a little louder than she might have if she wasn't meeting her niece for the first time in decades. I realised she was nervous too. It hadn't occurred to me that she wouldn't know that I was 'safe', gentle, that I came with no anger or resentment. We shared the usual preamble . . . how was your journey, I hope this cafe is OK, I'm dying for a coffee.

She didn't know that since I'd contacted her I'd been on a roller coaster. First teary relief that she hadn't ignored me or turned me away. Then, as our messages progressed, came painful, fragile optimism. I told people, 'I've been speaking to my aunt.' It was such a normal sentence, they couldn't have known what it meant to me.

To Peter I said, as we washed the dishes, 'You know, she's probably my nearest counterpart. I'm the "her" of the family. She got out, made a good life, had good relationships. She had to cut herself off too. If anyone will understand it's her.' But as the date of the meeting approached, I became wary. Peter had reassured me, 'Anyone would be so happy to have you as a family member. Delighted.' But now I was my aunt's Facebook friend I could see other photos; one of her and my sister, one of her and my mum cheek to cheek. The link to them made me uneasy. I thought again about Mark, about how that had hurt even though I'd expected so little of him, and I tamped down my hope that this might be different.

In the cafe I felt the easing, the warming, around the table. We exchanged news, questioning and answering, laughing too easily at poor jokes. Each of us saying to the other underneath the chatter, 'It's OK, I'm not here to harm you,' in whatever way we could.

Alison, though she calls herself Allie these days, showed me family photos accompanied by a description of the people in them. Pictures of aunts, great-aunts, my grandma, great-grandma. My mum's wedding to Richie. Me dressed in a pink satin bridesmaid dress at Uncle Mark's wedding.

Peter had only seen one picture of me as a child and leaned in. 'Look at you!' 'My God,' I kept saying. 'My God.' Those two words were incapable of quite expressing the off-balance, slightly nauseous feeling of retracing the planes and lines of those faces and forcing them into life and meaning for me again. My family.

One of the photos was of my mum at Uncle Mark's reception. I remember the run-up to that wedding. Trips into Sunderland to have a bolt of shot coral satin made into the world's most hideous bridesmaid dress, my mum searching charity shops for the perfect navy handbag that would one day contain the photos she'd rip up and throw in my face. Mum buying pastel- and black- and gold-coloured Sobranie cigarettes that she and Grandma ostentatiously smoked during the reception. She would have been thirty-four; the camera had caught her off guard, mouth slightly open in shock, her eyes wide. I hadn't realised that she was so beautiful. I hadn't realised she wore her fragility so visibly on her face.

'My God. That was the wedding when there was a huge row over an uncle swearing at the vicar.' We all laughed and I kept staring at the picture. Mum looked like she was about to cry. 'She was so beautiful.' I didn't add, I hadn't realised she was so obviously unwell.

Next came the family documents. Bobby used to work fixing submarines and then for the MoD. Now he'd tracked our family back through the decades. Out came a family tree. Ship manifests from the merchant navy. Birth certificates. Fragments of old addresses. He paused, held out a document. 'And what I discovered . . . was when your grandfather married Jeanie he was already married.' He paused again. 'He was a bigamist.'

I laughed. I laughed because I'd imagined much worse.

Speaking of her own withdrawal and eventual estrangement from Jeanie – her own mum, my mum's mum, my grandma – Allie said, 'I never knew if I was going to get the good Jeanie or the bad Jeanie. I used to say, "Call back when you haven't had a drink."'

She threw her hands up in the helpless way I also often do when trying to communicate the exponential complexities of my relationship with my mum. I understood completely. I was careful with my words. I didn't want to come between my mum and her sister who were also newly in touch by revealing too much but I did want to say, and for someone to hear, that there were reasons for what I had done. 'Without going into details about why I can't be in contact with Mum, it does seem like perhaps those cycles repeated themselves.'

I said nothing more, hoping my decency would speak the rest for me, that my nice manners and gentle way would come to my defence since my tongue was obviously still loyal to my mum, despite everything.

Some peace came to me then though, even as my body jangled

with caffeine. It was enough to partly understand. To see Mum in the context of the woman who terrorised her in much the same bewildering way that she made me feel constantly unsafe. It was enough to trace my fingertips over the patterns. It was enough to see in this woman in her sixties sitting opposite me, with her own eager-to-please demeanour, an image of my own self-preservation.

We talked about Allie and Bobby's kids, laughed about those terrible bridesmaids' dresses, our travels and Peter's proposal. As we were leaving the cafe I stopped to pet an elderly chocolate Labrador and then Allie had a go too. For a moment I wondered what I might have been had the universe delivered me into my aunt's womb. If I'd had the gentle Somerset childhood of her kids with handmade clothes, chutney and a mum I'd want to take part in charity 10ks with as an adult. But then I wouldn't be me and, though I sometimes find it hard to accept, me as I am is absolutely fine.

Peter and I headed alone to a local Wetherspoon's simply because it was the first pub we came to. It heaved with the after-work crowd and the whole place was full of hot breath, other people's words, the chink, chink, chink noises of a busy pub. My head felt too full, I kept shaking it, drank a half of ale quickly. 'I can't fucking believe he was a bigamist.'

Peter watched me warily, knowing it had been a big, exhausting day, checking me as you would a machine that's prone to glitches. 'It went well. They're nice people. Your aunt seems like a lovely person.'

I thought about when we'd said goodbye at the station and she'd held me tight and said, 'You have family now. You have an aunt. I have a niece.' And I'd said, 'I do. You do.'

I laid my head on Peter's bony shoulder. 'She is.'

9
Aberdeen
2018

Eventually I did make my second trip to Aberdeen. I went via Glasgow; there was a railway fault and the journey from Liverpool took me twelve hours. At every stop I considered cutting my losses and turning back. But I knew it was now or never and I'd no more money for tickets or hotels.

The next day, before travelling on to Aberdeen, I spent the day in Airdrie with a photographer, having my picture taken outside the buildings I'd grown up in. We'd caught the train together to the tiny town centre and then walked past the bleak shops and pubs that looked like they needed boarding up to my old estate. I stood outside a tenement, the wind lashing my hair, while I gazed into the distance at another tower block we'd lived in. There was something painfully intimate about me pointing out to the photographer and art director where I used to sleep as a kid.

'It was so damp and cold. How could nothing have changed in all these years?'

Still, I was in 'pleasing mode' and we laughed a lot as we took photos, my left trouser leg constantly intent on riding up. 'Sorry, my ankle was really looking forward to the shoot.' Between photo sessions we spent the morning and the afternoon in the local Costa talking about people we knew in common, our love lives, our jobs.

As we left the photographer, who had been so nice, turned and said, 'Well, I don't think it was so bad, growing up here.'

I nodded and raised my eyebrows. 'Well, thank you. I look forward to everyone saying the same thing when the book comes out.'

But afterwards, sitting on my Megabus to Aberdeen, woozy from a travel sickness pill, the comment kept coming back to me. Why make it at all? Was it meant to be reassuring? You're not as bad as you think? Or an assertion of his own ability to tough something out (though I knew, because we'd discussed it, he hadn't grown up like I had). Perhaps. I know it wasn't meant to be unkind. But it did make me think of all the other times that people who've no experience of poverty, of estates or disadvantage, inadvertently diminish the difficulty, the damage it does.

As the pretty countryside rushed by, lush greens and dark bruised purples, I realised, perhaps for the first time, why people say those things – because deep down they know it is an unfair system but to admit that would be to accept that they have contributed to and benefited from it. It would suggest that they've had perhaps just a small leg-up in life. And if they were speaking to me on a comparative equal level then how could they not acknowledge that privilege?

I thought of all the times someone had belittled me for not being quite right, when they came from where they did and me where I did, without acknowledging all the things that made their journey easier.

Suddenly I felt stronger than I had in a long time. Writing it, it seems so simple, but gently falling asleep to the Spanish couple's chatter next to me and the growling engine, I happily realised the game was up. From that moment I decided that, unless a person had grown up in the way I had, they didn't get to wade in with an opinion of it. I decided that I'd start to try to acknowledge the strength it had taken for me to get through, and over, my upbringing and become the woman I am today.

Behind the door of my Aberdeen B&B there was a yapping King Charles spaniel and a woman named Mary who looked so startlingly familiar, with her short-curled hair, delicate hands and face that spoke of plenty of booze and fags, that I almost asked her who her relatives were.

'It's £60 for the two nights.'

'Can I pay by card?'

'I've got to charge a pound if you do.' She held up her hands as though expecting a fight. 'There's nothing I can do, that's what they charge me.'

'No, no, it's OK. I understand. I'll go to the cash machine tomorrow.' And I did understand. I wouldn't needlessly lose a pound myself. Besides, I'd seen the 'For Sale' sign outside, and though the house was immaculate and warm it was a silent relic of the eighties and I was fairly sure that every pound counted at this stage.

She softened then. 'Are you sure?'

'Course.'

'What is it that you're doing here? You here for work?'

'I'm writing a book about where I grew up.'

'Where's that?'

'Torry.'

She raised her eyebrows. 'It's changed. You'll see.' She didn't say whether for the better or worse and I didn't ask. 'What school did you go to?'

'Torry Primary. I'm going to see that too.'

She smiled at me, just briefly, but enough for me to know it was hard won and I was grateful. 'You were booked for a small single, but *for my own convenience –*' she held up a finger, she didn't want to embarrass me or make it look like she was offering charity to me, a woman who grew up here but obviously had no family to stay with, who'd booked the cheapest possible room in the cheapest possible B&B in Aberdeen – 'I've put you in one of the twins.'

'Thanks very much. That's so nice.'

She shook her head. 'As I said, it's for my convenience. Because it's already all made up.'

The room was a perfect eighties throwback. Polycotton sheets, brown carpet, a little white kettle and ancient microwave ('so you can buy a ready meal from the shops if you like for dinner and save a few bob'), in the corner a small sink and a tiny Germolene-pink towel. The fridge was full of the miniature cereals I'd so coveted as a child and a pint of milk, there was tea and coffee and biscuits to feed a family. ('Eat as much as you want. Everything if you like. Let me know if you need more milk and I'll bring you another pint up.') I wondered how she could make any money on my £30 a night and then remembered her worry over the card fee and felt a sort of heat behind my forehead.

I pulled the curtains wide. The view outside was of a blue-hued mother-of-pearl dusk and neat rows of semi-detached houses, many of which were also B&Bs with vacancy signs in the windows. I microwaved a plastic container of carbonara and ate it contentedly in my pyjamas under the duvet while watching TV. The house was warm and quiet; I suspected I was the only guest. I thought of Mary downstairs with her dog and Saturday-night TV, maybe a glass of wine, and how unnecessarily kind she'd been. I felt a small, sharp pang. Perhaps this is what it's like to come home. Suddenly, I felt very lonely indeed.

The next morning, I saw no one and left the guest house in the direction of Torry. Nothing was familiar. There were nice houses and well-kept gardens, there were happy families enjoying their weekends walking their dogs and women pushing kids in buggies that I knew cost many hundreds of pounds – so different from the huge metal-framed, corduroy-upholstered prams that Mum insisted on for me and then my sister no matter that we usually lived on the top floor.

I walked along the wide river I'd no memory of and over a bridge that I did remember, me in tiny red wellies pelting away as fast as I could, thunk, thunk, thunk, while Mum shouted after me. That bridge separated me, and the shine and money of the city, from Torry, oil from water. And as soon as I was across and into Torry with its rows of dilapidated houses, overflowing bins and forlorn, cheap, grey net curtains that only a landlord ever chooses I knew I was home.

My walk changed. I felt it. Like I was growing. My shoulders broadening, steps lengthening, my chin slightly raised in challenge. Because, suddenly, I did know this city and it was mine. The Mackies had lived for centuries here and however prodigal I might be, my family had walked these streets before me and it was my right to walk them now.

I hadn't expected it, that feeling, a strange sense of sureness I imagine you only feel from knowing a place at your core and from earliest memory.

I walked past the old garage with its primary-coloured sign, maybe as old as me. Past Aitkens Bakery. It was closed and a sad letter in the window said it would soon be closed forever. I put my fingers to the glass and peered in like a little kid. The best butteries in Aberdeen came from this little bakery down a side street next to a garage.

Like Alice in Wonderland, I shrank to my tiny three-year-old self, eating a hot buttery out of a paper bag and smiling up at Mum because it was the best thing I'd eaten then or since. But just as quick I was an adult again, wanting to take that child in all her joyful glee and protect her forever, to give her those sorts of small kindnesses every day, to let her smile and laugh and feel well looked after. That kid deserved that. I took a deep breath, pushed those pointless thoughts aside and turned the corner onto my grandma's street.

It's a beautiful street. If you like your beauty utilitarian and some-what overbearing. A swooping curve of a hill with granite houses bearing down upon you. I remember the joy of that hill when I was little, how excitingly infinite it felt, like a ribbon unfurling. There, on the corner, was the old boozer we sometimes went to, the same dusty windows, the same many layers of tired snooker-table-green paintwork, the same impression of an uncertain welcome.

And there, on the other corner, the little shop I used to run to and buy a packet of Hedgehog crisps and Cadbury's Wildlife bars.

Grandma lived on one of the higher floors of her building. Mum would say, 'Just let me get my puff back,' pressing in her Adam's rib at the top of the stairs. I know it can't be the case but it seemed Grandma's little flat always smelled of roast chicken. I counted, over and over again, the 2ps I kept in a jar while Mum and Grandma called me 'Scrooge'. They would tie me up in my pants, with every belt and scarf in the house, and I'd pretend to be She-Ra and escape. For a while two Middle Eastern men lodged with Grandma and whenever I visited they'd give me a box of chocolates and once for Christmas a Barbie ballerina that spun around on a little stand.

Until I was about five my grandma doted on me. She wore knee-high, black leather boots and said if anyone gave me any trouble at school she'd go and 'kick them with her big boots'. She let me knead her huge braless breasts like dough while we both giggled. She had a 'crazy corner', a crevice where the arm had come away from the body of the sofa, where she stuffed everything – magazines, fags, lighters, glasses, Polo mints, tissues and the bottle of sparkling wine she had on the go.

In the way children will, I sensed her cruelty, her ability to be nasty for nasty's sake, not in my head at first, but in my belly. I felt an incomprehensible alarm in her presence. I was probably about ten when I started to really comprehend how she treated Mum and how, in turn, that affected our family. How much they argued, how often Mum tried to cut contact and Grandma won her back only to then punish her, restarting the cycle. I started to see how she was always claiming poverty – a utility bill that always needed paying that Mum was somehow meant to find the money for – but still always had fags and booze. She was probably the most hated woman I've ever known. While writing this I discovered not a single person with a good word to say about her.

I was in Prague when I heard she was dead. I'd just been to a basement gynaecologist to get my hormonal coil removed. The gynaecologist had been in her sixties, short and squat with a grey pixie cut and an incongruous white doctor's coat – except for the medical bed, it seemed the practice also doubled as her home. She had been warm and reassuring – not an easy thing to achieve when you're winching someone's vagina open with a speculum. I was still sore, still laughing with Peter about descending into the basement of a strange house in Prague to have a stranger mess with my uterus and how, as she'd removed the little piece of T-shaped wire, she'd shouted 'ta-da' like she'd pulled a rabbit from a hat, when I got the message from my sister.

It said, I think, 'Kerry, just found out grandma died.' Certainly, it was no more than a single sentence.

Peter and I went and drank some beer in a square that was incongruous in its golden sunshine and blossom-drifting beauty. I was weepy and shocked and strangely angry.

'She was a horrible woman, you know. She was terrible to everyone. And she lived till she was old. But she was still my grandma. Or maybe I'm just sad because I wish I'd had a different one.'

It would take weeks and many unanswered messages before I'd find out that she'd died some years previously from liver failure. Her ashes were scattered by South Breakwater Beach. Near death she would barely eat a bite, just smoked and drank and insulted whatever family was around. Apparently, the nurses at the hospital had all adored her, everyone thought she was a wonderful woman, and as she was being wheeled down the corridor one day she turned round and said to a family member, with a sour expression, 'See that? I've got all of them wrapped around my finger and it's all for nothing.'

I had no intention of returning to visit the place where her ashes were scattered. I was glad we were in Prague. It occurred to me that my constant travelling, from continent to continent, as far away as I could get, was not seeking but running.

But now I had chosen to go to Aberdeen. I stood for a moment outside the house that I thought might be hers. The sun shone, only to be absorbed by the dark grey of the buildings. Seagulls called, otherwise the street was empty. Even though I still wouldn't have dreamed of going to see where her ashes had been scattered, as I looked up I grieved for something in that moment, acknowledged a loss. I just didn't quite understand of what.

Jeanie Mackie's life had been hard and sad, this is a certainty. It would have driven anyone into a bitter place. But she'd stayed there too. She'd hunkered down and hurt everyone around her, often repeatedly. Her violet eyes hard and looking to wound. She died alone with only her fags and Lambrini, her pride and grudges for company. Funny, she always told me you reap what you sow.

*

I turned off the GPS on my phone. I knew exactly where to go. Around the curve was the beginning of the estates of Torry, squat blocks with faded red balconies and those sad, unused squares of grass that count for communal space on estates. I stood in front of the Balnagask Road house where my great-grandma, Florrie, lived. Did I really stand in her kitchen while Mum drank tea, Florrie surrounded by her grizzly true-crime magazines?

I've always found families who live only a few streets away from one another a strange breed. I've always wondered at them all, dropping into each other's houses willy-nilly for tea and gossip and spontaneous – stretched out with a few tatties – dinners. It's difficult to imagine I came from a family like that. That if we hadn't 'disappeared' – as I'll be told we did – I might have spent my childhood and teens running between one or the other of their houses, fetching them shopping and listening to their stories and being rewarded with a rare 50p piece. Except we were never that sort of family.

Our family was mercurial and fractured, one relative told me. I also found out that in the nineties the family was given genetic testing because of the inordinate incidence of schizophrenia among the past males of the family. The results came back showing a genetic disposition to the condition and that parents should ensure their children were mindful about drug and alcohol use. We also had an unusual amount of bipolar disorder among past women but they didn't test for that. On top of this, at least half of the much older generation of the family had been undeniable alcoholics, while the rest 'liked a drink' as one cousin put it. When you add family dynamics, poverty and all that comes with it and close-knit community, no wonder they never stood a chance.

The air changed, the seagulls cried louder and I found myself at the Bay of Nigg. I loved a walk there with Mum. It wasn't anything special really, just some rocks and little beach. It was always blowing a hoolie so there was no paddling or burying myself in warm, damp sand. But it was a time for me and Mum, and we only did it when she was in a good mood. I still remember her walking about so confidently in her jeans and sweatshirt, her short hair, and me feeling proud and mimicking her. I remember my glee, my absolute, pure love for this woman who had taken me to smell the sea.

Everything was so much smaller. That this is a terrible cliché doesn't stop it from being right. It had always felt miles to the Bay of Nigg but it was less than ten minutes. In fact, nothing – Grandma's house, Great-Grandma Florrie's, the sea, my flat, my old school – was more than twenty-five minutes apart. It amazed me that I had once lived in such a community. That I had over twenty second cousins, and even more of their kids, running about Torry. That I could have bumped into relatives going to the shop for messages or walking to school. That I could have said 'I'm a Mackie' and people would have known what that meant and might have gone to school with someone from my family. Mum probably left for exactly that reason.

Our estate looked the same. I didn't remember the huge Dee-side Family Support Centre on the edge of it, though, and had read that the Eastern European community of Aberdeen had relocated here, so it wasn't entirely unchanged. Mum used to tell me I should run to the shop and back as quickly as possible. That it was dangerous. The alleyways and closes did seem menacing then – with their broken bottles and ripped open, overflowing bin bags spitting out shitty nappies and household detritus.

It still looked poor. There was a lone bus stop at the edge of the estate. An old woman and a young mother with a child in a buggy waited. I remembered doing the same with my mum, though more commonly we would 'hoof it' and save the fare. Perhaps that's why the shining city of Aberdeen, then and now, didn't seem familiar to me. I hadn't really been born in Aberdeen, Torry was a country all of its own. I wondered what might have happened if some of the oil money the city had seen had been reinvested in Torry over the years. If the residents there had been given some of that shiny gloss and sense of prosperity. How different would it have felt to grow up like that? What might the outcomes have been for kids who grew up believing their city thought they deserved a decent environment just like everyone else?

The communal washing poles were still rising up from the ground and I remembered running through them like a maze, screaming as clothes flapped in the wind and I got more and more lost. There was the landing, a walkway along the block where I had ridden my spacehopper, pretending to be a Scottish cowgirl, wearing the same cowboy hat that had sat skew-whiff on Grandma's head in that picture from my third birthday.

The few people who were around, taking out bins or bending over an open car bonnet, viewed me with suspicion. I had thought that perhaps I would feel threatened, but instead I felt that they viewed a stranger as the threat, so I did my best to say hello and smile. I noticed one young woman in skinny jeans and a collection of drapey scarves who looked at me curiously as I sat on a bench typing notes into my phone. She was carrying groceries and a bottle of red wine and looked exactly like the sort of person I might befriend if I lived here now.

Next, I walked along the street of little prefab houses all built on a slant that Grandma called the chicken coops. Behind them I could see the huge field that I was never to go in alone. I suddenly had a memory of Mum doing an impromptu firework display there, taking the fireworks out of a biscuit tin and making all the kids hold hands and pace backwards together until we were at a safe distance. It seemed so at odds with my mum's usual behaviour, for so many reasons, but the memory was there.

And us walking home from school through that field while she told me we were going to San Diego to meet my American grandma. That my dad would pay for the tickets and maybe we'd never come back. I could hear the breathy, delighted voice of my Grandma Millie on a payphone and there was the parcel she sent with little plastic cups and a coffee pot that magically refilled with black coffee. I had found in my dad's flat years' worth of birthday and Christmas cards from my grandma to me saying 'please give my angel girl a kiss from me', 'I think about my beautiful grand-daughter every day with tears in my eyes' and always a request for a few photos. My father never passed these on nor, as far as I know, sent the photos. He was angry with his mother until she died from not being able to afford medical care or medication in San Diego. There seems to be a lot of that kind of anger in our family.

I walked up the long row of those chicken-coop houses to my old school. I used to pick the berries of a snowberry bush and throw them down so I could pop them under the soles of my school shoes. For a while Mum met me, gave me a little treat and walked home with me, and for a while she didn't, and I was left to meander home alone. I can't remember which preceded which, whether things got better, or things got worse.

Now, I peered at houses, garden ornaments, net curtains, bins overflowing, neat hedges. One of the doors opened and a young guy walked out, probably no older than twenty. He wore a baseball cap, a polo shirt, a pair of baggy joggers. He had that hard, hungry expression I knew from the men I'd grown up with. He looked up, met my eye and, in that moment, I caught his full assessment. He was seeing if I was fuckable or a threat or something useful before he realised I was none of these things. He walked his way and I walked mine. I didn't blame him. It was natural. It was how you survived. Hyper-vigilance always. Looking for pockets of comfort or relief or gain or for things that might suddenly, violently explode. I'm sure I do it now without even knowing it.

I saw my school in the distance, a squat building that you reached down some steps, the strangely art deco rounded front, and all of it in that same oppressive dark grey granite. A gate was open and I smelled the chlorine before I saw there was a new swimming pool – Tullos Swimming Baths – attached to the school.

I walked around the empty playground. When I'd told Mum that we played a game called kiss chase where the boys also pulled our skirts up she told me not to play that game any more, that no one was allowed to touch me, especially not boys. I brought in 2p pieces to exchange for a length of paper to thread through a huge paper chain that coiled along the school corridors like a rainbow snake. I was fairly happy at this little school, feeling mostly safe as I often did in schools, at least until I got older.

It felt somehow magical that I could be standing now in the place I once stood when I was only four years old. Obviously, I could have got on a train or bus and come at any time but, even so, it seemed miraculous to be standing there as a grown woman, with all the things I had done and seen, remembering being so small and sweet and mostly blank, playing kiss chase and hopscotching up and down those bright, painted squares.

On my way back through the playground I passed a small, slightly dilapidated area with a picnic bench. I watched a woman, maybe a little younger than me, with her child who couldn't have been one yet. It wasn't anything special, they were sitting on some boulders in the sunshine and the woman was just talking gently, almost in a whisper, to the pink-clad baby who leaned and squatted against the boulders, took little plodding steps and rocked on her heels but never fell. I looked over and smiled at them and the woman smiled back briefly and then returned her gaze to her child. It was only a second, but I felt something move within me looking at that mother and child in my old place, looking at a long-gone past and my possible future all at once.

I was hungry by now but to eat I would have had to walk twenty-five minutes to a huge retail park with an Argos, B&Q and Asda, and if I wanted to eat well I would have had to walk all the way back to town. It had started to rain by then. The insidious soft drizzle that soaks you through before you realise. In the whole estate I couldn't see one cafe or shop. Only a bus stop midway showing an advert for American Express – a woman in white jeans sipping an espresso outside a pavement cafe in Paris. I walked on and fumed at the insult of having an advert like that up in a place like this. Yes, I was sure people had credit cards on the estate, terrible ones with ransom-like interest rates and bailiffs on speed dial, but they'd be used to pay for food, electric bills, to fix a broken washing machine or for school shoes. I was thinking of every time I was reminded growing up that there was a whole world out there that I couldn't begin to imagine, that people were living and enjoying, while we counted our pennies to see if we could even afford the bus or would have to walk through the rain again.

Except, of course, I had been to Paris. So many times, I'd lost count. I'd had my book published there and won that fancy prize. I'd been on the TV and in newspapers and there was a big party held in my honour with lots of champagne and tiny éclairs and canapés. Afterwards, we went for dinner and the restaurant magically found us a good table and brought more free champagne. My agent was paying and, worried her expenses had a limit, I ordered the cheapest thing on the menu, an onion soup.

I briefly thought about going back and trying to take the poster out of its display on principle. But by then I was walking over the river away from Torry and was hungry and tired. I went to a hip cafe decorated in bleached wood with kombucha on the specials board and had a vegan scone and an Americano and worked for a while on my Mac. Torry seemed so far away then, my anger over the daft advertisement a bit embarrassing, the two parts always wilfully separate. Water and oil.

10
Canterbury
1986

We took the National Express down to London before we got to Canterbury. It must have been a gruelling journey for Mum, with her life's possessions in a few cases and a whining, frightened kid to drag along behind her.

While we hadn't had much to part with, it was my first taste of the idea of simply abandoning the things that made a home and life: the plates we ate our chips off, the big pink plastic mug Mum bought in a failed bid to stop me spilling my hot sugary tea, those beloved orange velvet curtains that even in adulthood I'm still searching for. My grandma, my uncle, my school and my pals – all suddenly gone.

I was learning about impermanence, that everything was expendable. That you could wake up from one morning to the next and find your life had changed completely.

On that endless coach ride down to London we stopped at some motorway services and an older man bought us a tartan travel blanket. My mum recounted the tale many times over the years – 'Still with the tags on. Brand new!' she'd always say, and we'd both stop for a second and think about how decent he was. The mythical One Good Man. To see a young mum and her kid sleeping on a coach like that and want to make their journey that bit easier, it must have cost him a lot of money, a brand-new blanket, and who had money to throw around like that when you were taking the coach yourself?

I don't recall that first visit to London. But I seem to remember the taste of lemon meringue pie, the crust of sugar on my upper lip, the tang on my tongue. But this might also be a memory stolen from another time.

What I do know is that when we went to my dad's last known address – he had many at any given time, usually belonging to friends or girlfriends – Lynne, his current friend/girlfriend, wasn't happy to see us. She put us up for the night and then turned us away.

Whether Dad was hiding from us or simply not around we never found out. He specialised in appearing and disappearing at will and was never there when he was needed.

For my birthday that year he'd sent me a huge tome of poetry, an expensive black woollen cape, and other ridiculous, unsuitable presents for a young child. Those gifts spoke of lots of money and no knowledge of me at all. And why would he have any when I never spoke to him on the phone, never saw him from year to year?

Eventually we ended up on the coach to Canterbury, I suspect largely because that's where we could afford a ticket to.

At some point on that trip down from Aberdeen, Mum took us to the local Sally Army and told them we had nowhere to go for the night. She told me the 'ugly, fat ginger fuck' just shrugged, got her a pile of blankets and sent us on our way. After that Mum would never give their bands a penny on the street even if I really wanted to. I don't remember that night or the blankets.

When we arrived in Canterbury I stood outside the phone box and watched as my mum called B&B after B&B from a Yellow Pages borrowed from a nearby shop and somehow, miraculously, found us somewhere to sleep.

I thought she was nice at first, Mrs Stone. A character from a story like a fairy godmother or a nice witch who saved us from sleeping outside.

She was a child-woman. Smaller even than Mum's five foot nothing, though she was much older. I thought she was bird-like before I ever knew the term. She gave the impression that her whole body was made of waxy, delicate sticks like the wishbone of a chicken I would snap with my pinkie with Grandma after Sunday lunches. Small, dark, shining eyes that never rested, a plume of stiff, blow-dried hair.

Mrs Stone laughed a lot, her head tilted, and always looked nice in her pastel suits, like a woman off TV. Even when she wore jeans she looked dressed up, with a lot of jewellery and a perfume that the room smelled of long after she'd left.

After the dreariness of Aberdeen, that tall, grand house on a proper street in Canterbury was like going to live in a TV programme too.

I remember Mum sitting on the bottom of the bunk bed that took up half the room looking up at Mrs Stone while she ran us through the rules and I inspected the breakfast tray with its cling-film-wrapped pieces of bread and irresistible tiny boxes of cereals.

We were forbidden to be in the house from 10 a.m. to 5.30 p.m. and there was a 'top-up' fee that would need to be paid from our social money in addition to our housing benefits. Mrs Stone would personally deliver the weekly breakfast tray we would also need to pay for.

I'm fairly sure it was at this point that my mum started to see Mrs Stone was trying to fuck us over.

I could hear the familiar growl starting in my mum's voice, the tightening of her mouth that meant she was about to 'blow'. Even thinking about it I have that panicked feeling in my belly. I understood nothing except that I wanted to stay in that warm room, to sleep in bunk beds with my mum and eat some of that dolly-sized cereal. I didn't want to go back to the phone box or another coach or another cafe where we couldn't afford anything but a drink. I wanted to stay in this story, this miniature room, belonging to this miniature woman with miniature breakfast food.

I didn't understand that Mrs Stone with her gold rings and hair like Alexis from *Dynasty* was shafting us. I didn't understand that the crappy little breakfast tray she appeared to take so much pride in would cost us double, maybe triple, what it cost her and would, with the added extra rent, gouge out everything but the most basic things, and often those too, from our benefits, already calculated to be the littlest amount we could subsist on. I didn't understand how empty and boring those long days would feel when we were forced to be away from that little room, or how hungry you could get when your mum didn't have enough to buy snacks because you'd already paid £2 for a slice of cling-filmed bread, a pat of rancid butter and a tiny box of cereal you'd eaten too quickly that morning.

I didn't know how it would hurt Mum to hear me complain about those cold, tedious days or how starving I was or thirsty or to hear my pleading to go back and get a toy or watch the TV.

But I'd learn quickly enough and stop.

I didn't understand when, after a few weeks of being there, Mrs Stone brought me a pile of neatly wrapped birthday presents and Mum said in a fury, 'She bought those with our money. Those presents are really from me.'

I came to understand though. Years after we left that B&B, Mrs Stone became our household pantomime villain. Even a decade later we'd occasionally sit around our little four-bar electric fire and call her a bitch. Mum told me in my teens that Mrs Stone had been exposed on *Watchdog* for being a slum landlord. Sadly, I haven't been able to find any evidence of this. Perhaps it was wishful thinking. I could have done with seeing her get her comeuppance.

Canterbury was my first experience of those who 'have'. Mrs

Stone had. She had somewhere for us to live and that meant she had power and she chose to use that power to gain more money and more power while also, as she benevolently dispensed presents with her tinkling laugh, making sure my mum and I were ground a little further down in the social order.

I don't know how we adapted to living in that small room together. I remember Grandma appearing for my birthday, bringing me a make-up kit, with a bright pink bullet lipstick as a present, and then leaving again just as suddenly.

I was six now and learning all the time. We found ourselves pitched even further down the helter-skelter of depreciating living standards. We were no longer living in a flat of our own with our own furniture in a city my mum knew with family around us. We were on our own with a few suitcases to our name and poorer than ever.

I think my mum naively assumed that with a small kid she would simply be given a council house. And why wouldn't she think that? The news said all the time that that's what single mothers got. But in Canterbury they told her she'd made herself 'voluntarily homeless' by leaving our Aberdeen council housing without notice. As far as they were concerned, we already had a 'home' at Mrs Stone's (though I think that word is a stretch for bunk beds, a sink and a travel kettle).

From the earliest age, almost before I knew how to write my own name, I could recite to you the intricacies of the housing and benefits system. Terms like 'points' (meaning how many housing points you had which correlated to how soon you'd be rehoused), 'top-ups' (the amount you'd have to find in addition to housing benefit) and 'voluntarily homeless' just became part of my vocabulary. Mum told me everything and I asked questions, absorbed language, learned like any child does.

I don't know how long we stayed at Mrs Stone's flophouse. I

know I started school and then, I think, left for another. We moved to a second B&B further out of town which seemed cavernous after Mrs Stone's. Every morning we'd get up and have a fried breakfast with the other tenants – a woman who'd had cancer, a fat older man from London, a young woman who gave someone a kidney ('that's fucking weird' was Mum's assessment). We still slept on bunk beds but in a bigger, sparser room.

My memory of the place is of how institutional it felt; grey Formica, the smell of detergent, the milling sense of people just killing time, of big mugs of metallic tea and the first taste of fried bread on my tongue. Every morning I'd run down and the fat man from London in a slightly dirty T-shirt who cooked up the breakfasts would give me an extra slice.

When we moved on again, to our final Canterbury B&B, I cried because I couldn't have fried bread any more. Funny, I can't stomach it now.

There is a hierarchy of temporary homeless accommodation. A shit scale. At the bottom was Mrs Stone's which, while clean and warm enough, was in every other way designed to squeeze the guests as much as possible, to reduce their days to simply trying to survive the experience. Our next was like a hospital waiting room you had to sleep in with a cafe that only served fried breakfasts (though at least they were included in the rent). Our third B&B in Canterbury moved us up on the shit scale. Yes, we were still living in one room at the top of the house, nothing in it but a double bed and single camp bed for me, but the house had a little garden where snowdrops grew, there was a park nearby that we'd walk to, and a fish and chip shop with a glowing orange light that I'd run into asking for a bag of 'scraps' (the batter bits scooped from the bottom of the heated glass cabinet).

The B&B was run by a man called Majid who Mum seemed to like. In the kitchen we had our own cupboard for food and a Busy Lizzie plant I was allowed to water each morning while Mum spent her time at the communal table chatting with the other guests. I was the only child and people indulged me, said I cheered the place up.

Things seemed better. Certainly, I've happy memories of playing in the park, stopping at the deli on the main road and buying a few slices of ham with flecks of pepper in them and eating them from the wrapper, of jumping from the kitchen counters and playing throughout the whole house just as if it were my own. Mum bought me some *Twinkle* annuals and a few cuddly toys from a charity shop and for months I was Nurse Nancy, caring for my dollies and for my pale pink rabbit with its stained fur and chewed-up plastic whiskers.

Like a child's soft, malleable bones, bendy until they break and are glued together again without complaint, even if it's not quite at the right angle, I simply adjusted my idea of 'home'. Maybe it involved lots of people, not just me and Mum. Maybe it was our little room, after all, that just meant I was closer to Mum.

The hints that our life was not rosy came from others. The class's reactions when the four or five of us who got free school dinners trooped up to get our green tokens, a sense of shame blooming in my belly before I even understood why. Making friends with the boy who lived in the house next to the B&B, whose family of three lived in the same space as many, many grown adults. They had a big biscuit tin of sweets and one day I convinced the boy to take some for us. When his mum found out I could see the varying pulls of emotion on her face – I was no good, a bad influence, I was just a kid, a poor kid who lived in a hostel. She asked me, 'Did you steal these because you were hungry? If you're hungry you can always come here and ask for a sandwich, we can give you dinner, but you can't steal.' But I hadn't stolen because I was hungry. I'd stolen because I was a kid and there was a whole tin of sweets in a cupboard and what kid wouldn't?

Not long after that the boy stopped coming out to play. That was the first of many times that I would watch my friends' parents eye me over and dislike what they saw.

Mum got a cleaning job, cash in hand. She'd take me with her and I'd lie on my belly and colour in. Going to that house – so clean, plush, so full of light – was like visiting a different planet. The woman, 'call me Gillian', was decent to Mum, I'm sure she wanted to reach beyond the boundaries of their different places in society.

Gillian once took me with her nephew to see a middle-aged blonde woman in concert, perhaps Elaine Paige, and then to a proper fancy restaurant to eat a chocolate bombe. Somehow a wine glass smashed for no reason on the table and, though I hadn't been near, Gillian and her friend looked at me as though I'd done it with my mind. 'You're sure you didn't touch it, Kerry?' If I'd been older I might have asked if their own sense of guilt at their meagre show of liberal benevolence had in fact been to blame.

Gillian wandered about her gleaming house with its many floors, the bathroom polished to a shine by my mum on her hands and knees. Still, at the end of those days Mum was given a few clumsily folded notes and we went back to our six square metres of home grateful for the money. And I suppose they were as much friends as people can be when one pays the other to clean their toilet.

It was around this time that Mum started taking her 'sleeps'. She could sleep for hours. I understand it now as depression, the weight of the hard last few months bearing down and the knowledge that she could finally rest knowing I was in a safe house. I see why she chose curling up under a candlewick blanket in her jeans and T-shirt. I just carried on, playing my dollies' hospital game, making up little conversations between me and my toys, lining up my colouring pencils over and over again until the early evening when Mum would get up.

When she woke up I felt like the luckiest girl in the world to have her attention again. She would smooth down the pillow-mussed angles of her hair and take me to the park. I still remember that high, how I'd keep opening my mind to her in the way children do as I slid from the top of the single slide that made up the playground.

His name was Richie. He didn't dress like everyone else. He wore only khaki tracksuits. He seemed like a giant, though I know now he was just an averagely tall man. We always met him smoking his little grey-worm roll-ups in the kitchen where he took up manspreaded residence. He was not a handsome man, he had bad teeth and a big nose, a curly bush of blond hair. But he was Scottish and self-assured and had a way with words. He could be a charmer, a joker. He sang to my mum – 'I dream of Jeannie with her light brown hair.' They played gin rummy, he'd get Mum to share a drink with him. It must have been good to have the company, the attention.

'He'll take care of us,' was what Mum said. He liked to make sure we knew he was ex-army. He ran in the mornings, which was why he always sat around for the rest of the day in his tracksuit. It seemed he'd barely arrived and then he was always there.

He eventually got a job delivering meat and he took us out with him, driving the scenic route to a park so I could feed the geese. There was suddenly a freezer full of meat and Mum would make huge Sunday roasts for everyone in the house.

Majid moved out of the B&B and we moved with Richie into his vacated studio apartment on the ground floor with its wide double doors to the garden. It felt like a palace after our little room at the top.

Richie drove us to a blackberry-picking farm where you paid by the basket. He hid a whole punnet inside his canvas hat, red juice dripping down his sweaty face as he stood in front of the weighing counter, while me and Mum looked on, our legs crossed so we didn't piss ourselves laughing.

I had my reservations about this strange giant though. He was strict, he told me off even though – we were all clear on this – only Mum got to do that. His favourite saying was that children should be 'seen and not heard', along with 'never give a sucker an even break'. He'd often say, 'I'll never lay a hand on you,' as though he deserved a medal. He drank all the time and so Mum did too and I hated it when Mum drank.

At some point, my dad visited briefly and gave me an antique child's violin. I took lessons at school, my hands in a claw shape trying to reach the little orange stickers, but it wasn't encouraged at home. Eventually it was pawned for a few twenties. I got a fake Barbie, with a hollow orange body, and a tiny tea set with thimble cups from the newsagent's in its place. Mum and Richie drank and smoked well for a good few nights.

It had just been me and Mum and now there was this man with his particular ways and his strong opinions about disciplining a child taking up all the space and farting and making jokes at my expense.

Still, Mum had a job with someone she liked, she laughed

more and stopped taking those long sleeps. We had our little flat, I had some friends at school. It felt like home. A sort of home anyway.

They didn't tell me they were getting married, they simply announced I was getting a new dad. Richie was perhaps only in his thirties when my mum and him met. But to me he seemed so much older. He had been brought up in a strict house with a timid mother, brothers who he drank and fought and played practical jokes with. He'd worked manual labour jobs his whole life, had been in the army. He had his ways, liked to think of himself as a matinee idol. He used Brylcreem to slick back his blond curls and would never shelter from a downpour. Instead, he took pleasure in turning up his collar and strolling slowly, 'cool as a cucumber' he'd say, past crowds of people cowering in shop doorways. He loved Laurel and Hardy, classical music, crosswords, chess and cards. He wanted to be a writer and was often found with his tree-trunk legs splayed around a charity-shop typewriter, typing with two huge index fingers with bitten-down nails. I think he wrote my mum poetry.

He could be kind. He could, when he chose to, be patient with Mum when she was having one of those days where she careened. I understand why Mum might have clung to him and his rigidity, his old-fashioned and black-and-white perspective on everything, as though hanging on to the biggest bit of wood in a shipwreck.

Here are some things he also liked. He liked cheating when he played cards, even if it was with his six-year-old stepdaughter. He enjoyed getting something for nothing, or out of people who were stupid enough. Running. Smoking and drinking and gambling even if it was our food money he used. Stubbornly refusing to budge if he was in the wrong. Getting jobs and then leaving them because he couldn't be bothered.

I called him Dad like Mum wanted me to but we were locked in a constant power dynamic, the three of us. Him wanting to be the head of the house, wanting respect. My mum wanting a strong man but never having honoured or obeyed anyone in her life. Me, wanting a daddy, wanting my mum to be happy, wanting it just to be the two of us again, resenting this stranger suddenly telling me what to do.

I think they got married a month or two after they met. It was quick, anyway. I don't know how they found the money but I remember the engagement ring was pawned and bought back even in the few months we remained in Canterbury. They married at the registry office in the presence of my grandma, Richie's tall, skinny, silver-haired brother, Stewart, my Auntie Allie, Gillian and a few people from the B&B. My mum wanted people to wear shades of aquamarine for the wedding party. Her and Grandma rowed about it. Years later when we talked about that day Mum would say, 'And she couldn't, even for one day, just do what I asked.'

Gillian drove us to the registry office I think. Or maybe it was just a taxi. There was a ribbon tied around the car. In the only picture from the day, taken by Gillian, Mum is in a second-hand turquoise pencil dress, a little baby's breath flower in her hair. I stand at her legs in a little pale green two-piece suit from the market clutching my china doll (another extravagant gift from my father who'd yet to pay any money towards food, clothes or housing), squinting into the sun. I still remember how stiff the little suit was, how special I'd felt in it as I twirled around, the polyester pleated skirt rustling like it was whispering to me, probably saying 'avoid naked flames'.

Mum looks beautiful in that picture. So young and slim, like a model, smiling right into the lens, full of hope. My new dad stands with one hand in the pocket of a beige charity-shop jacket, his shirt a little tight around the belly, roll-up in the other hand. He's smiling too, a knowing half-smile, looking like he just got away with something. The same face I'd soon get to know when he was winding me up about something, or when he'd marked the cards we were playing gin rummy with.

After the wedding, there was some sort of buffet back at the B&B and everyone brought a bottle and squeezed into our little studio flat. There had never been so much food and I crammed my mouth with crisps and mini sausage rolls. Gillian came back too and perched uncomfortably on the edge of the sofa. She hadn't brought a bottle (something often pointed out when talking about that day), but she did bring a present, a marble board with a wire to slice fine cheeses. As though we regularly bought a wheel of Brie for after dinner. We took it on all our moves (after trying and failing to sell it) and sliced our big blocks of sweating mild Cheddar with it for years after.

I enjoyed the pop and the sausage rolls, my new Uncle Stewart sang and played the guitar. My Auntie Allie, who had a lovely voice, sang too, though under duress because she was always shy about it. The afternoon wore on, booze seeped into everyone's limbs and the arguments started. At some point my little china doll got smashed. I had to sleep with Grandma when I wanted Mum and was fucking furious about it.

Me, Mum and Richie left Canterbury and the B&B not long after the wedding. As ever, there was little warning of the move. I don't know why we left. Maybe Richie wanted to be close to his family. He'd already been sacked from his job, so it wasn't that. Perhaps it was the inevitable, gossamer-thin promise of a 'fresh start'.

We loaded most of the B&B furniture into the back of a rented van. I remember my outrage. In my child's mind it felt like taking from family. My new dad laughed uproariously. 'We'll need to toughen her up.' He'd say that a lot over the next few years.

I learned a new term, 'moonlit flit', as we barrelled off into the night in a van stuffed with furniture, and catalogue coats for the winter and school shoes for me, a *War of the Worlds* tape we weren't going to pay for on the stereo, me arguing because I wanted to be on Mum's lap.

Richie loved to drive and took the scenic route all the way. We slept under duvets in the back of the van and ate a lot of crisps. I remember a strange deserted pub with blood-red walls and a mounted stag's head. At some point beyond Newcastle my mum realised that we should probably be on a motorway and not on a country road with views of sweeping hills, since it made the journey so much longer, and made him stop the van. She screamed that he was a selfish bastard and they were finished.

But what choice did she really have? She was in the middle of the countryside without a penny to her name. She was also pregnant with his baby.

We all got back into the van and by the time I'd eaten a bag of cheese and onion crisps they'd made up and we kept going on that wrong road, barrelling north.

11
Liverpool
2018

Two weeks before our wedding we got a tiny black kitten. I was lonely at home and wanted something to love. We named her Dora since, though she could fit in the palm of Peter's hand, she wanted to explore every inch of our flat. Then on 12 April I got married to Peter at Liverpool Town Hall. Just the two of us and two dear friends as witnesses. I wore a £25 dress. We laughed – 'Big knuckles,' I'd mugged as I struggled to put Peter's ring on – and cried our way through the short ceremony in the smallest room at the top of the building. We had baked a Persian love cake ourselves and gave out slices of it along with little plastic cups of champagne to other passengers on the train to our honeymoon night in Wales.

I had always slightly dreaded a wedding day with the conspicuous absence of my family. But in the end, I had everything I needed right there.

My favourite moment was putting on my make-up in the hotel bathroom mirror the next day. Peter came in and poured me a cup of coffee from a silver pot. He put a hand around my waist, gave my neck a gentle kiss and then walked out again distractedly to continue packing. We hadn't said a word, but I knew that we belonged to each other. Never had I felt something so solid under my feet. So warm and right that it reached every part of my body.

12
Canterbury
2018

I arrived in Canterbury on a National Express coach just like I had over thirty years earlier. The coach spat its passengers out in a congested bus station in the centre of town and, since one of the many things that I've discovered hasn't changed in the intervening decades is coach toilets, I walked straight to Fenwick department store. It was jarring being somewhere so shiny – full of designer make-up, handbags and face cream that cost as much as my rent – after the coach which, as everyone knows, you only take if you're scrimping. You just feel hard up when you take the coach, as though thriftiness is pumped through the spinning-eye air conditioners that whimper out tepid air. In adulthood, I've often been ashamed to admit that I've arrived somewhere by coach – like not being able to stretch to a train ticket was proof of some moral failing.

Outside the Fenwick toilets stood a gaggle of teenage schoolkids, their ties loosened around their necks, standing by a reconstruction of a living room: a pillar-box-red L-shaped sofa, a chrome-and-glass coffee table, enormous TV and an expressionistic painting of a field of poppies. Most of the kids were clustered in on themselves, chatting over each other, one scrolling her thumb across the bright rectangle of her phone screen. But one boy held back, his hands in his pockets, staring at the furniture. One of the girls called over to him and he joined them, shaking his head, 'Imagine living somewhere like that.' And with one final backward look he left with the other kids.

I watched him go, my heart like a stone under my ribs. Because I could see, just in the way it takes one to know one, that he didn't come from a home where the wealth of a shop like this felt like something within reach. Perhaps, though, I was projecting. I knew well enough what it was like to imagine others' lives, the simultaneous wanting and hating. I considered going after him, telling him he could have anything he wanted but that the poppy picture was God-awful and to remember money couldn't buy taste.

I let my phone lead me to my Airbnb which was advertised as a 'bohemian hideaway'. There was a sense of déjà vu as I reached a complicated roundabout I couldn't figure out how to breach. My feet were guiding me along a long road. The last time I thought of that road was when I was in Vietnam writing my first novel and I reimagined it as a road *squeezed tight with off-licences, betting shops and kebab houses.* And while the shops might have been a little nicer – one sold only decorative furniture knobs – it was unmistakably that street. There was the chippie, and perhaps that was the deli where Mum would go in and buy five slices of salami for pennies and, yes, there was the antique shop where Richie continually tried to sell anything we had of any value including, I think, my little violin.

Amazed by the coincidence of booking a room in my old neighbourhood, though I'd had no idea where that was, I ignored the insistent buzz of my phone telling me which street to walk. Like a bloodhound, I turned up every side street trying to find our old B&B, the one where Mum had her wedding reception and where we waited out the Great Storm of 1987 sitting in the kitchen, eating food from the freezer and using the gas oven to keep us warm.

Sweating, pulling my suitcase behind me, I turned quickly onto one street and then another. But they never looked quite right. I found myself, red-faced and dishevelled, peering through windows and standing on steps to see if those could possibly be the steps that me, my mum and Richie had stood on with mugs of tea watching swifts cut through the sky. Richie had turned to me and said, 'They're flying through the air with their mouths open eating beasties,' and I'd replied furiously, 'No they're not! They're just enjoying having a fly.'

I was already half an hour late for check-in when I finally obeyed my phone and made my way through the streets to my room. It was indeed fairly bohemian with intense paintings of nudes and piles of dusty coffee-table books.

That night I went into town for dinner. Although I do remember finding Canterbury beautiful as a child, certainly more so than Torry, my enduring memories were of our B&Bs, those scruffy streets and the park Mum took me to in the early evenings with its lonely slide that was its only nod to a playground.

As I walked the cobbled streets, browsed menus at bistros and looked in the windows of endless chichi craft shops, it seemed inconceivable that this was once a part of my childhood. Except, of course, it wasn't. Mine was asking for scraps at the fish and chip shop, amusing myself during interminable waits at the benefits office and creaking metal bunk beds used by many homeless people before me and Mum.

I went to a cafe decorated with swathes of velvet, fat armchairs and gilt mirrors and ordered a Parma ham flatbread with a balsamic reduction and a pot of Earl Grey tea. But it all stuck in my throat. I wondered how different my life might have been if I'd grown up among this beauty. In a place like this with two universities full of young, bright people who were going to do things with their lives. I wondered how it would have changed my perspective of the world and the future. Why would Mum move us from a place where it seemed there was so much opportunity and possibility to North Lanarkshire which even back then was in rapid decline? Possibly it was because Richie wanted to but then I think of that boy yearning for his Fenwick's living room. I think of the LSE psychologist I once spoke to who said that comparison was the root of dissatisfaction. That in an experiment the same people could feel richer or poorer just because of where they sat on different income spectrums, their income never changing only the brackets above and below theirs.

In fact, 'studentification' is an ongoing problem in Canterbury. There are, of course, huge benefits to having two thriving universities for both the city and its poorer residents – the boost to the economy (long-term employment is better than the national average), the energy bright young things bring, the likelihood that at least some of them might make it their home, and the fact that the youth vote probably secured the first Labour victory in Canterbury in a hundred years at the 2017 general election.

But the very tangible difficulties are also clear. Canterbury has the lowest rate of owner-occupied housing in the UK at 43% and a local vice chair of a prominent residents' association, David Kemsley, recently said he believed there were nine hundred unoccupied houses of multiple occupation (HMOs) in the city while there were over two thousand names on the council house waiting list. It's not hard to see why families, like my own, living in temporary or shitty accommodation might come to resent students, though, of course, it is the landlords and universities who really bear the blame. Students have to live somewhere but keeping houses empty in the hope that student tenants will materialise means available, cheap housing is tied up while people languish in a limbo of statutory homelessness. The other issue is that many student houses don't pay council tax and they don't usually have children resident and neighbourhoods respond to them and their money – so primary schools close and nightclubs open. And often, though not always, they are not as engaged with a local community they know they are only borrowing.

Certainly, the stats from the 2017 Health Profile from Public Health England tell their own story with alcohol-specific and self-harm hospital stays, violent crime and statutory homelessness all higher than the national averages.

Perhaps Mum had been smarter than I realised. Because in Airdrie we might have been in the shit but at least mostly everyone was in the shit together. And there were always council houses to be had in North Lanarkshire, because no one else wanted them.

I gave up on dinner, walked back through the city's booming, boozy Saturday night to my room with its ram skulls and fleas that kept jumping on my socks and slept the fitful sleep of someone far away from home in all ways.

The next morning, before breakfast, I decided to walk up the street to see what other memories emerged. It was a beautiful day, a bold, blue sky overhead and sunshine lighting up every surface.

I heard the children before I saw the gate. Inside there was a clearly brand-new playground with everything you could wish for: slides of every length, a multi-part climbing frame with nets, tunnels and hidey-holes, three types of swing including a flat circular one to lie in looking at the sky, wooden bobbing animals and a zip wire.

In the centre of the park was the trunk of a felled tree, four or five foot wide, on which someone had placed an apple. I put my hands on the warm wood. I had known that tree well, I'd run around it, played games under it and laid my head in my mum's lap under its dappled shade. I walked to the now empty spot where my slide used to be. I don't remember any other kids in that park, just me and Mum, that ancient sheltering tree and the rusted green metal slide with the dents of children's heels down its shiny silver length.

I sat for a while under a tree watching children playing, mums dragging buggies from one area to another, one eye constantly on their kids, one hand always free and hovering though they let them climb with abandon.

Perhaps, I thought, as I left the park and emerged onto the busy road that had once made up my whole life, I must accept that it's possible to be many things all at once.

13
Airdrie
1987

My first impression of Airdrie was of wet greys and mossy greens and a scrum of a town centre, a tightly clumped collection of shops and cafes that were always steamy from tea urns and full of cigarette smoke.

My mum and I were welcomed uneasily into the family. Richie's closest brother, Stewart, who'd come to the wedding, skinny and tall, with pale blue eyes, a Lanark Paul Newman, lived in what Richie called his 'bachelor pad' a few streets away from their mum.

Stewart was often unemployed, loved cards and booze like his brother. Richie once got him to cut off his trouser leg in a wager. His little council flat had a full wall photographic mural of a watermill in a forest in the living room.

Their mum's flat, my new gran's, had the very same layout as Stewart's, a tiny living room, a bedroom, bathroom, a little box of a kitchen and a long, thin, seemingly always frosty back garden. But 'Grannie Pat's' smelled of rich tea biscuits and overcooked veg.

When Stewart had his watermill mural put up he'd got one of a tropical beach sunset put up in her living room too, complete with palm trees, lapping turquoise waves, and mango-and-watermelon-coloured horizon. When I arrived, I thought it was the best thing I'd ever seen. I used to lie on the thin, musty-smelling carpet in front of it and pretend I was sunbathing, that any minute I'd jump up from that small cold room and run into the waves. Writing that now makes me feel fairly triumphant that, as an adult,

I have done exactly that on many a far-flung, tropical beach, as though my wanting it so desperately made it true.

There was another brother, Bruce, the eldest, with a proper job doing something important, maybe in the gas or oil industry. 'Loaded' is how Richie and Stewart used to describe him. They called him 'the big yin' but there was a sense they were also a bit fucked off with him for having what they didn't.

We stayed with Grannie Pat initially, all squeezed into her flat. She must have been in her seventies and, looking back, I imagine she had early-onset dementia. She was deeply religious and had a face twenty years older than her age, deeply lined and improbably tanned – like a crumpled paper bag. Her dentures were bright white and her hair wisped around her head in a halo. She had the air of a mad scientist who'd retired to Florida.

She was a gentle, quiet woman. Her sentences were often fragmented, descending from very quiet to whisper, trailing off but followed up with an expression that begged you to simply understand and free her from the torment of forming more words.

She'd taken to cutting up anything that was lying around – cushion covers, her own clothes, tea towels – and sewing them back together again. All of her dresses had been cut in half and then reattached with long wide running stitches – as though she might be a craft project herself. One of the biggest rows Mum and Richie ever had was over her cutting apart and resewing Mum's 'wedding towels'. Mum was sure it was malevolent, 'she knows exactly what she's doing', but Richie countered, 'She sewed them back, didn't she?'

My stepgran was delighted to have a kid in the house and to have her wee boy back again. Perhaps she was less delighted when she found out that I largely said and did whatever I wanted, that 'seen and not heard' was an oxymoron for me.

She was certainly less happy to see my mum, with her short kitchen-sink haircut, jeans and jumpers, her swearing, drinking, smoking, her big laugh and even bigger temper. My mum permeated the atmosphere with a sense of rebellion. My mum, who had run away to London, who had lived in squats and loved punks and had funny ideas about the role of women, who already had a difficult mother and didn't need another who disapproved of her, wasn't cut out to live in a strict Catholic's house. Those women were not meant to occupy the same small flat. They weren't even meant to occupy the same era.

But she was kind to me, Grannie Pat. She'd always go into her purse for a shiny 20p; she showed me how to make oatmeal, a smooth, salty disc floating in sugared milk. She took me to Communion perhaps hoping it wasn't too late for me.

God knows where we all slept. I assume me, Mum and Richie took the double bed and she slept on the sofa. Slowly, me and Mum fractiously occupied that world of pan loaves and egg, chips and beans. Of 'not taking the word of God in vain', of Richie going off to Dillets pub or the betting shop or Stewart's for a drink and cards. And Mum wanting to be there too but having me and so being stuck at home waiting, worrying about how much money was being spent. Of Orange Lodge marches and a new benefits office. Of frequent rows between Mum and Richie. Of going to the park and choosing Celtic or Rangers when quizzed and not knowing why the wrong answer would see me chased home. Of cold that felt like it stripped the top sheet of skin from my legs. Of 'scrambles' after weddings where kids from the local estate would wait outside churches for the bridal party to throw pennies and scrabble to catch them, pushing each other out of the way. Of understanding, just as Mum did, that we'd gotten ourselves into a small, cold, grey box that didn't fit at all. Straight into a traditional, Catholic, patriarchal family in a town where we knew no one and understood nothing about how or why things happened the way they did.

My stepdad kept saying to me, 'You know your problem? You're too sensitive. You've got to toughen up.' My mum picked this call up, too, eventually. And I was, it was true. I was too sensitive for the knee-jerk violence of the estate, the shouting, the scrabbling for coins whether there was a wedding that day or not. I was too sensitive to grow up in a house where my mum was deeply, desperately, furiously unhappy with a man I thought resented my being there as another mouth to feed when that money could have been spent on Buckfast and fags. I was too sensitive for the playgrounds and the kids who made fun of my funny accent and my clothes.

Outside and inside it seemed I was at odds with everything. The options seemed to be to cry or fight or disappear. I cried, and I fought, and I raged all the time. But at least I didn't disappear.

We moved to a sublet council house that belonged to a friend of a friend of a friend. I don't remember much about it, the usual four-bar fire, sour-smelling brown carpet, second-hand furniture from the decade before. There were carved wooden stag ornaments that became my favourite toys. I do remember there was permanent stress about being discovered and made homeless, that there were lies to learn about why we were living there. I started one school and then got taken out when we got our 'permanent' flat. And what a flat it was.

There is a big difference between living on an estate when you're a toddler, or three or four, and when you're seven. Until you're five the world is a tangle of confusion and delight and everything can be made better by lying in your mum's lap, placing your head on her chest, inhaling the smell of her that represents home. The days pass in a jumble and anything bad is felt in one surging high pitch and then forgotten with a chocolate bar or a nap or a TV programme – or at least they seem to be forgotten. That I'm writing this book suggests those staccato high pitches of emotion burrow down somewhere deep, waiting their turn until decades later.

When we arrived in Airdrie, if I fell, if I was hungry, if I was scared, if I was excited by something, I still ran to my mum. But once we moved into our flat it felt like I had been given glasses and the things that had seemed indistinct, the things that I could only make out the vague shape of, suddenly became clearer too. The glasses had an imperfect prescription because I still couldn't understand the detail, the construction, the composition of things, but nonetheless I started realising that everything was not OK. That perhaps Mum wouldn't simply always protect me. In fact, I might need to protect her.

Our new flat was at the top of one of the many tower blocks in Balquider Court in Holehills, which was surrounded by places with names like Thrashbush. 'Hellholes,' my mum used to say, 'Thrushbush!' and she'd throw her head back and laugh while Richie sat stony-faced removing a speck of tobacco from his tongue with those big fingers of his. Something else he wanted was his woman to be 'ladylike'.

While writing this, I found an archive picture of Balquider Court and the concrete bin house next door that I can still smell – something animal, mulchy, dying in my nostrils. The blocks are smaller than I remember. Not the high high-rises of my memory, grey fingers reaching to the sky, but lumpen buildings, perhaps only six or seven storeys.

Our flat smelled of fresh paint and old smoke from the fire which had displaced the previous tenants and given us somewhere to live. Mum didn't want to take it, so, for reassurance,

Richie nailed a huge coil of orange nylon rope to the wall by the window.

'How will that work?' Mum asked.

'We throw down blankets, mattresses, use the rope.'

'We'll kill ourselves.'

Richie turned to me smiling. 'A few broken bones never hurt anyone.'

The flat felt fairly big, after Grannie Pat's and the other place, but no one wanted that flat at the top of a block where the lifts never worked and with the bin house right on your doorstep. The lift was graffitied and smelled of piss. One of the landings always smelled of disinfectant and I feel sad to think of the woman, for it was surely a woman, who came out each day with her bucket desperately trying to hold back the deterioration of the building and the area around her.

Boys would go into the bin house with old tennis bats and planks of wood and whack away at the little birds that nested in the rafters. Mum used to go down and shout at them. I was so proud of her for that, I thought she was so brave. Richie never moved from his chair and his little knee-high table laid out with his cigarette papers, tobacco, his Buckfast drank from a tiny glass like it was a fine French wine.

They demolished those bin houses in the late eighties apparently. I assume because of the vermin and the fact they were a sanitation disaster. It's a fairly damning indictment of a slum to have mounds of rotting waste right in the middle of six housing blocks, like a decaying front garden, where children play.

Not long after we moved into Balquider Mum's belly started to swell with the baby. I started playing on the estate where the Rangers and Celtic question was still the most important one you could answer. I made some friends, I went to school. I took to skip diving and found a half complete 'make your own teddy bear' set that I used to sew bright orange faux-fur costumes for my Barbie. I danced to Yazz at birthday parties. I wanted to be a dancer/fashion designer.

We got tins of meat with no labels and huge blocks of cheese from the back of vans that came round the estate if we showed our benefits books. Richie came swaggering in with them as though he had a prize deer over his shoulder, but Mum refused to use the meat, saying you had no idea what muck was inside them. We used a big bottle of Fairy Liquid to clean our hair, bodies, clothes, house and dishes. But we had a record player and a Betamax video player that Richie would watch *Rambo* on, an undulating line of static cutting the screen in half.

Richie and Mum rowed more than ever. He disappeared regularly, often for days at a time. Sometimes there would be money – if Richie won at the betting shop – mostly there wasn't. I learned to parrot my mum if I was out with Richie – 'Mum said you shouldn't spend money on betting. Mum said to get bread, she didn't say a Pot Noodle.' A wee wifey myself, nagging and as pissed off and impotent as the real thing.

My grandma came from Aberdeen for a visit late on in Mum's pregnancy but left abruptly after a few days of everyone drinking together. Mum trying to paint a room for the baby, them all drinking into the night and Mum screaming they were ganging up on her, 'thick as thieves'. Perhaps the paint was thrown across the room, perhaps that was another time. I think Mum thought Grandma was flirting with Richie. Certainly, I wouldn't have put it past her.

Eventually I got a little sister. A little bundle with beautiful blue eyes. Mum stayed in afterwards to have her 'tubes tied'. When she came back from the hospital I was to be entirely silent, not to disturb her at all. Richie lost his temper with me more and more.

Now I can see that my stepdad was a man panicking at the weight of his responsibilities set starkly against his need to think only of himself.

I was seven when she came along. I loved my sister. I used my pocket money to buy her lollipops knowing she couldn't eat solids. I ran home from school each day, so I could give her a feed. I treated her like my own little dolly. One day she slid from the bed and got a carpet burn right down the front of her nose that stayed for months and so we called her Cherry Nose from that point on.

There were signs, so many, that things weren't right in the house, but when you're a kid you mostly feel it in the stomach aches you get for no reason, in not sleeping, in knowing you're hungry but shouldn't ask for something to eat again.

My mum was called away to the funeral of her Uncle Robert, an alcoholic, who, if family lore is to be believed, went drunkenly to the children's home to try and give money to the kids sometime around Christmas, was turned away by the staff and was hit by a car walking back across the road. This was the closest thing my family had to a martyr story and everyone was devastated. She came back, as she always did from seeing her family in Aberdeen, ashen, exhausted and clearly, even to a seven-year-old, unwell. Of course, there had been some argument about something during the funeral. I've never known a family like mine for fighting. As though they were fighting for life itself.

While Mum was away Richie had lost our benefits money, and so we went to the social to get a crisis loan. He said it had slipped out of his back pocket. Mum threw the whole big pot of potato curry, meant to be our week's dinners at him. It didn't help anything but who could blame her.

I think in those days she simmered with fury, disappointment, sadness. I don't know what the neighbours or my teachers saw when they looked at me but what they should have seen was a family imploding, struggling, barely hanging on.

Richie left properly for the first time when my sister was still in her first year. He walked out in the middle of the night, leaving us with nothing but a long walk to the benefits office to ask for yet another crisis loan.

The benefits people were right about one thing, it really did seem there was always an emergency in our house.

We moved to yet another flat on another estate in Airdrie, though close enough that my school stayed the same. This flat was on the ground floor. I assume we were given it because Mum was a single parent and couldn't be expected to manage the stairs loaded with shopping and the big old-fashioned pram she had for my sister.

It was an old building and the winter was brutal. Wet slid inside the window frames, black gunk collected there, damp climbed up the walls. And the glossy paint Mum found on discount only made it worse. All drying after a bath, all changing, all eating and activities happened as close as possible to the four-bar fire in the living room.

Mum started baking from a library book with little bags of flour and sugar from the bucket shop in town. For a while there were always little French biscuits or cake. You'd never imagine us council estate kids eating delicate, home-made sugar-coated palmier biscuits in our damp flat.

We had a lovely Christmas tree that year and had acquired a black cat we called Squeak 2. My dad visited and things seemed to be going well. We all had a spaghetti fight that seemed hilarious, so funny, until halfway through Mum started crying and raging that we'd made a mess, though she had initiated it in the first place. He only stayed a day or two but ensured he was remembered fondly in the form of a pair of white leather fringed cowboy boots that, for a while, loaned me some popularity with the other girls.

I don't know when Richie came back. I can't remember if he stayed with us or with his family. I only recall the row. Mum and him standing in the dark empty car park of a pub, each screaming my sister was theirs, me screaming at them to stop until some other adult pulled me to one side. I remember, in that rough pub on the edge of a rough estate, the shock etched onto the onlookers' faces. I knew it was bad because it took a lot to shock around there.

Another time, not long after that, when Richie had gone once again, Mum had a night drinking with the upstairs neighbours. Afterwards we'd come back down to our flat and were rooting through the biscuit tin that only had broken digestives, maybe a Nice biscuit or two in it. I was, as I always was, furious at my mum for her loss of control, her slurs, her wobbling head and big, big laugh. I felt ill in my stomach. I threw a little biscuit at her, shouting, 'You're drunk.' And she laughed so I threw another. I laughed along and threw another and another and then, just like that, she hated me.

She told me I was a selfish little cow, that I was a nasty little bitch. She snarled at me, too drunk to raise her voice too much. 'Go on,' she said, 'get out. I'm done with you.' And I'm sure I shouted back, that I hated her, that she was horrible. 'Oh, you hate me, do you?' So she dragged me upstairs to the neighbours. I was weeping by then, bewildered.

The neighbours opened the door with a smile they dropped like a stone when it was clear this wasn't a social visit. My mum declared she was done with me. They could take me until social services came the next day. Come on, they reasoned with her. No, she was done, I was an ungrateful little cow.

Behind the neighbours their kids stood in their pyjamas,

shocked. Humiliation swept over me in a hot wave. In the end the mother ushered me in, gave me pyjamas. The kids asked me, maybe in the morning or that night, full of the horror of the idea of a child simply being given away, 'What will happen'? And I replied, 'I don't know, she doesn't want me.' 'What about your sister?' And I shrugged and said again, 'I don't know.'

My mum came the next morning, face pale and hair slicked back from a shower. She apologised to the neighbours and took me downstairs to our flat. She said she would never hurt me, that she loved me, that she wouldn't ever do that again. I must have asked her not to drink any more, I always did. But I can't remember what her answer was.

It wasn't long after that that I came home to find Mum packing in the usual frenzy of energy that came with a 'new start'. We'd got a postcard from Richie, with his thick biro block writing on the back. He was in North Shields. It was a 'great place!' with 'loads of work!' So, we packed our bags and got on another National Express coach to another place.

14
Airdrie
2018

The Love N Light Recovery Cafe was housed in a church a few streets away from Airdrie train station. I'd been browsing the community Facebook group for Airdrie and had come across Bill and Julie's cafe.

I walked there directly from the station, keen to avoid facing my past for another hour or so. Airdrie had the same low-lying, rain-swollen sky I always remembered and there was something comforting about that. When I walked in I saw a woman wearing a red T-shirt saying 'RECOVERY' on the back and a slightly harassed look. 'Don't leave your bag out,' she said. I assumed she must be Julie. When I started to approach her she held up her hand and shook her head.

'Talk to Bill. I'm off into a women's meeting.'

A large man wearing a North Face jacket and a thick gold necklace with a praying-hands pendant, appeared. His hair was shorn, he had a face that had clearly seen some life and bright blue eyes that insisted on constant eye contact. He introduced himself. I explained that I'd lived in the area as a child and was talking to people about their experiences for a book I was writing.

Bill spoke with a thick accent but quietly for such a big man. The first thing he told me was that he was a recovering addict himself, 'a former cocaine, heroin . . . everythin' addict'.

I asked him how the cafe had started.

'A committee of people identified there was a need in North Lanarkshire. For families and children who'd been at the wrath of addiction. It was recognised no one was doing anything for them. I believe this is meant to be. I believe in the universe, in God, whatever you want to call it. I believe this was divine intervention.'

I became uneasy as I always do with religious people. I don't want to have to spurn their well-intentioned soul-saving advances. But he said he didn't think of it as religious.

'If you want to use a label then we'd say spiritual. But we use the word sparsely within the community because it's not a word used that much. Spiritual in the sense of anything for the greater good of others or your community.'

He toured me around the small room, introducing me to some volunteers, two teens, one with Barbie-pink hair, the other with braces, both wearing the same bright red T-shirts. Every Saturday, from twelve to four, the Love N Light serve breakfast for families affected by addiction and offer workshops, maybe some music or entertainment. There were trestle tables set out, one for self-help literature focusing mostly on the Twelve Steps, 'the recovery library' they called it, another with a woman knitting intricate newborn baby clothes that she gave away to whoever needed them, another was loaded up with donated loaves of supermarket bread that visitors could take home.

Outside by the entrance where it was quiet Bill told me it wasn't just about supporting people with addictions but their families, too, in a bid to break the cycle of dysfunction. I nodded. 'I lived in a family where addiction of various kinds was a real issue. A lot of writing this book is about the dysfunction that carries down from generation to generation and how that can be stopped.'

For a moment we were both silent because, between us, we'd seen enough and knew enough to fill in the blanks between my words and understood all the things that a simple sentence meant. For one mortifying moment I felt the pressure of hot tears forming and took out my phone to take a picture of their banner. Bill watched as I took pictures I didn't need. 'We understand – 85% of the volunteers here have been there. We get it.'

He spoke in a rapid monologue and I interrupted where I could to make sounds of agreement.

'You can talk till yer blue in the face about the problem but we live in the solution and the gateway to that is to push through the shame. You know, you can live for forty years with shame and die with it or go through two minutes of shame and come in and say, "Can you help me?" Thirty seconds to say, "I've got a problem." So it's forty years versus two minutes.' He said they were trying to deal with the issues related to living with addiction as early as possible for the kids. And working with their parents to identify and tackle the root cause of their problems. 'What's happened is we've gone into an epidemic of heroin addiction. And life's got bigger and faster and more. With Universal Credit coming in it's going to get bigger. People like us, who're looking for a hand-out to help these people, are told they don't have any money. So it leaves a lot of charitable work to be begged off folk who are begging.'

He walked me back to the cafe where people eyed me, perhaps curiously, perhaps a little suspiciously despite the fact Bill was right by my side. He told me that every year they send families who wouldn't otherwise get a break on retreats where they learn skills to help them recover. They get addicts to write their past down on a long scroll of paper and then throw it into a bonfire on the last night – 'writing is therapeutic'. How can I possibly disagree? He surprised me by telling me he was trained to deliver Tibetan healing sound baths.

'Oh, I had one of those once. In Dharamshala in India. It was lovely but I fell asleep.'

But by then he had moved on and gave me his card so I could

send him some advice about writing a recovery book. I told him I'd do my best and wrote down my details too. Julie, now out of her meeting, shouted over, 'Is this yours?'

I'd left my computer and purse in a neat, showy little pile on the entrance table. 'God, it is.'

'Didn't I tell you to watch your stuff?'

'You did. Sorry!'

I gathered it all up as she watched on shaking her head.

'We're addicts here, you know. We don't need that temptation.'

She was joking, at least partly anyway, but I still apologised and then said my goodbyes.

When I left I wanted sugar, warmth and quiet, like someone who's just given blood, and so went to a cafe down a backstreet with a wall of novelty salt & pepper shakers. I ordered a Twix and a cup of tea in a mug with a parrot for the handle. I felt so moved by what they were doing at Love N Light even if the religious element of the Twelve Steps was something that sat uneasily with me. Airdrie couldn't have been an easy place to encourage people to look at their habits, certainly not the Airdrie I'd known. And they were just normal folk who'd seen something that needed to be done and had done it. It made me feel, for all my travels and career accomplishments, like I owed a debt that I hadn't even started paying yet.

I climbed the hill from town after that, towards the tall towers. Through the old estate, the houses far the worse for wear, black crows hopping from roof to roof. It was quiet except for a few kids playing, a woman pulling her child up and down in a slide on shallow snow along a slope. I smiled as the kid shouted at her to go again and she threw her hands up in the air. 'I didn't think this through.'

My old estate now had something called a 'concierge', as though they might get you into a good restaurant or arrange theatre tickets. This is what they laughingly called the security guard who sat in a squat red-brick hut monitoring who should be allowed through the electric gates. I'd learn later that this was a new initiative on troubled estates. Cameras everywhere and control of who came and went. But the concierge was nowhere to be seen and the gates were wide open, so I decided to take my chances.

I walked along to the spot where Richie had taught me to ride a bike. Considering he thought the way to teach someone to swim was to just throw them in at the deep end, I actually don't remember it being too bad. It was the same spot where I'd waved Grandma off after her disastrous visit for my sister's birth, when she was so full of righteous indignation.

I didn't like being there. It was very quiet but I had the definite sense that I was treading a fine line by being inside those gates. That my usual smiling and claiming heritage and nostalgia wouldn't cut it.

Ahead of me a guy in a tracksuit, his face still rough with sleep, leaned into an ice-cream van to talk to the man inside. When they saw me they both stared hard until I averted my eyes, as I'd learned to do from an early age, and walked in the other direction. I wondered how often that ice-cream van was let in through those big electric gates.

I spotted a man on his way into the estate and asked him where I could catch a bus back to town. I'd stopped him because his matching mustard-yellow beanie hat and scarf made him look daft and safe. Up close I saw he'd red-veined skin, the beet nose of a drinker. I recognised it well enough in my own family. He asked me where my accent was from and I gave my usual line about being a 'mongrel' who had picked up bits of accents from everywhere. He told me he had two daughters who spoke with Irish accents.

'I used to live here in the eighties. It was pretty rough here back then to be honest. What's it like now?'

He smiled. I got the impression he was glad of someone to speak to, someone listening. He told me he'd been OK. 'I had a few eejits round my door and I said –' he raised his voice – ' "You fuck off away from my door." '

I gestured at the gates and the fucking useless brick hut. 'This works OK then?'

'They can't do anythin'. There's CCTV from the door to the outside. I'm fine anyway. I've the top floor in the corner, I just keep to myself and no one bothers me. Ma brother calls it Trump Towers.'

I laughed and we waved goodbye.

I had one more stop. Down the hill, away from those tower blocks, following a map my eight-year-old brain had drawn for me. I saw two kids, a brother and sister, struggling with a hyperactive collie puppy and stopped to pet it. The pup jumped and jumped, barking and licking at the little boy's face.

'Does it love the snow?' I asked.

He grinned. 'He doesn't love the snow. He just loves me.'

Around the corner was St Serfs, my old school, where we'd Hail Mary and Our Father six times a day and were taught we'd probably still go to hell. Where I learned to confess my sins and sat in the supply cupboard while everyone else learned about First Communion because Mum didn't believe in religion. One kind teacher had bought me a velvet colouring-in picture of a dinosaur and a big pack of felt tips when I cried because everyone else got new dresses and presents for their First Communion.

I walked up the hill towards our fourth home in Airdrie. Big grey tenements with new metal chain link protecting the ground floor where we once lived. The hill was knee-deep in snow and my feet were sodden, the freezing air bit at my face and the sun bleached out my vision, but standing there, outside that home I had few happy memories of, I felt a sense of elation.

I walked over to the single rusting goalpost outside the tenements. I used to swing upside down from it while wearing my beloved white fringed cowboy boots. Now it barely reached to my chest. I touched the cold metal for a moment saying a little thank you that it was me as I am now who was coming back to this place instead of all the other versions I might have been, the broken versions of myself I could easily have ended up as.

On the train back to Glasgow I searched Twitter for the word 'Airdrie' and read tweets about 'alchies', and there being 'no soap', about 'drug deals', and never wanting to go to Airdrie.

I'd felt that way myself, but I didn't any more. It wasn't the place or the people that made it hard. It was everything else feeding into and off a small, deprived town like Airdrie. It was notorious and forgotten simultaneously.

Within half an hour I was back in Glasgow but I might as well have travelled to a different continent. I felt a bewildering, powerful flush of loyalty and anger on behalf of the decent people in that town, doing their best, as life just got harder.

15
North Shields
1988

I don't know what Richie had promised but what we got was an industrial town on the bank of the River Tyne. He'd found us a private rental in a row of red-brick terraced houses. It was pretty compared to what we'd left. For a while there was a semblance of peace. Richie taught me to play chess, we played cards, he still cheated but less. We had no TV, because Richie despised them, and no microwave either, because he said they filled food with radiation.

We had furniture, acquired from somewhere, and a nice park nearby. It wasn't too bad. But then it all fell apart, Richie was suddenly gone again and we had to leave that house and go and live in a B&B.

The B&B was huge and almost opposite my new school. The other guests were largely older men. It was essentially a homeless shelter. There was a cooked breakfast included but eventually Mum got them to knock that cost off our rent because she didn't like us eating with the men.

We had the top room with its sloping ceiling, bunk beds, one camp bed and a tiny rectangular window. Behind a plasterboard divider there was a mini-fridge, a little plug-in frying pan and a sink. They called it a studio. There were communal showers for 20p a go, so we had two a week until we figured out we could sneak in and shower quickly after someone else had paid. Mum guarded the door.

The 'managers', a young couple who always seemed to be cuddling, wore matching baggy jumpers and lived on the ground floor. They had a huge board with a list of films on and I would go down and pick either *Footloose* or *Dirty Dancing*, or both, which would then magically appear on our TV at the top of the house when you flicked to a certain channel. I watched them over and over, dancing in front of the TV, above the heads of all the other tenants whiling away their day, the floorboards fairly shaking. Or I did until the other guests started complaining that they were sick of those films and I was told I could only have them once a week.

That was the year of the first Comic Relief on telly. Mum wanted us to watch it all the way through and I wanted to be friends with all the children. We ate a lot of Scotch pancakes with jam and tinned cream, and sausages with mustard. My sister, not yet two, and I sat inches from the TV screen.

I could walk to school across the road and through the park. The school was small and had a strong emphasis on, of all things, cricket. The kids learned I was from Scotland and called me Loch Ness Monster.

Later in the year some of them learned I lived in a B&B. I suppose most walked by it on their way to school. I denied it. They followed me home one day and, when I failed to lose them on the backstreets, I picked a nice-looking house with a conservatory, went all the way to the door and then hid in the back garden. When the owner came out and asked what I was doing I explained in a rush of words and tears then ran away in the face of her sad comprehension.

My dad was in contact and still paying maintenance in the form of expensive presents. The latest was a very plush, full-size cat cuddly toy simply named 'Black Cat'. I was probably too old to be carrying it around but I was attached to it and was always delighted when someone pretended it was real.

Richie came back, yet again, and crammed his huge frame into our little room too. And so, the drinking, smoking and arguments started up again, until he left, just as suddenly as he'd arrived. My sister was still too young to understand these changes in our daily life, toppling around with that giant head of hers, unaware of what should be and what shouldn't. Just as I had been until that year when reality slowly started seeping into my anxious wee bones.

One night, in the early hours, all the residents of the B&B were evacuated. We huddled together on the pavement, me with a towel wrapped around me in the blue flash of the fire engine.

'He says he's going to burn the place down, mad fucker.'

I stood mutely staring up at our window, thinking of our few possessions, worried I only had vest, knickers and a towel with me. It emerged that the man had been holding his lighter under the smoke detector, had locked himself in his room and had to be coaxed out because he was threatening to set the whole place, and himself, alight.

Of course, anyone could end up living next to someone with mental illness but that was the first time I realised our home wasn't a safe one. I suddenly understood why Mum didn't want us playing in the corridors, why she guarded the door to the shower room. I knew then that it couldn't be right to live in a house of strangers of whom we knew nothing except that, like us, they'd somehow drifted right to the edge of society.

16
Hetton-le-Hole
1989

'Hetton-le-Hole? As in *hole?*' Mum had asked and perhaps the man taking us in his car laughed. The man from the housing association had come to see us in the B&B. I saw Mum telling him about how bad it was and piped up, 'And we've to pay 20p to have a shower.' Mum shushed me – 'Whisht.'

I never understood the rules for when it was OK to say the truth about how bad things were, when we should pretend otherwise, and to which adults about what things. Even at eight years old I could see him trying to keep the shock off his face as he took in the shabby room, our tiny grimy window, the rickety beds. When he left, out the flimsy door and down the stairs past all those other doors with all those other people behind them, Mum turned to me and said, 'That went well.'

And a few days, or maybe weeks, later we were in his car and on our way to see a house. A house! A proper house! I hadn't been in many cars, maybe the occasional taxi. This man was smart, he wore a clean shirt, he smiled nicely when I chattered on. My sister and I sat in the back seat looking at his own kid's picture books while Mum and him sat companionably in the front. I secretly wished that he would be our new dad.

It wasn't actually a house at all. It was a second-floor flat in a little red-brick house on an estate of other little red-brick houses in cul-de-sacs. I suspect at some point in the early eighties it was meant to be the height of good social housing design. Interspersed around the cul-de-sacs were raised gardens filled with shrubs for looks not for playing. Us kids skinned our knees getting up into them anyway.

Where the estate ended, a few minutes from our house, there was a scrubby bit of land with a swing set, some fenced-in horses and allotments. Through a narrow makeshift dirt path by the allotments you would reach rows of terraced miners cottages and, walking down the alley behind them, you would find yourself at the cricket club and then, finally, there was the thirty-minute walk down, up and down again (for Hetton was literally in a hole) to town.

Hellhole is what Mum would call it. But that day Mum, who always longed for the city, didn't say anything. Except maybe that it was very 'quiet' or 'out of the way'.

There was a sudden cooling of relations between Mum and the man after we'd seen the house and the estate. The jovial, 'going on an adventure' atmosphere had been replaced with something else on the journey back. Perhaps he thought she should have been more grateful. Perhaps he was disappointed she was disappointed. In the back seat my mind was full of thoughts of having my own room and those ponies (in fact, fat, old horses) that I was sure I could learn to ride, my fingers tangled in their manes.

We moved into the flat with nothing. Mum got a maintenance grant to furnish the house. I think it was around £175. With that grant, which sounded like such a lot of money to us when we never had a spare £5, we had to buy an entire household of things. Every plate, pan, knife, bowl, a fridge, a cooker, a sofa, beds, bedding and towels, somewhere to keep clothes, a bath mat. There's no room in a grant like that for pictures, cushions, rugs or toys. Nothing to make a place homely or comforting.

Soon after, there was another grant for school uniform.

There was no uniform at my school, so Mum had to fight for the money. She was always so good at fighting. I sometimes think, in another world, she could have made a great City trader or perhaps a divorce lawyer – something that would have allowed her to use that terrier instinct to bite at the slightest provocation and never let go.

Not having school uniform was, in retrospect, progressive for a school in that area at that time but Mum still had to find clothes that would make me look presentable at school every single day. The shabbiness of my clothes would show us up.

Mum took me and my sister shopping in Sunderland and, favouring things that would last, knowing that the next grant was a year away, bought me a navy knitted skirt and jumper from BHS and a nice patent leather raincoat on sale. Her idea was that these would be my 'uniform'. So, when I started school, the new girl with the funny accent, I wore the same clothes every day for two weeks. I repeated what Mum had said, that it was my uniform, that I had other clothes to wear outside school, and when I got home they went straight into the washing machine (partly true), but the kids said I smelled. That nice black raincoat (which as an adult I would love to own) won me the nickname 'Bin Bag'. After that second week I came home, took everything off and stood furious in my vest and pants saying I wouldn't wear them again.

Hetton Lyons Primary was a small and close-knit school. My teachers were all good and dedicated. I felt they cared for me. The head teacher, Mr Green, took particular interest in helping me by giving me little jobs, making me feel special. It was both an old-fashioned school with its own traditions (cross-country running, country dancing, the maypole, the brass band) and straining to be progressive (the non-school uniform, a drive for environmentalism when it was still seen as 'hippyish', teachers who played guitar

and taught us protest songs). I did better at that school than anywhere else in my education. But I couldn't stay there forever.

When we arrived in Hetton-le-Hole the very final mining
jobs were being fought for, the last of the pits closing. So, though
we were poor, and conspicuously so, we still existed within a
working-class community who understood poverty and treated it
with compassion. My mum was given a big bag of clothes by
another single parent who lived on the estate. I was delighted with
the oversized Nike T-shirts and wore them over a pair of threadbare leggings for my whole school year.

They'd been through the strikes and the lay-offs, they knew
how grinding and unexpected poverty could be and they also knew
where the real blame should be directed. I was aware of the fact we
couldn't afford much, that every penny had to be considered, but I
didn't realise there was a spectrum of poverty. At least until it was
time for another school tradition: the annual spring trip. A kind
teacher, who had taken an interest in me, got the school to agree to
pay for me to go so I wouldn't be the only child left behind.

She made the offer discreetly to my mum, who in turn acted
pleased and grateful. But she was neither pleased nor grateful and
didn't want me to go. I wouldn't have the same stuff as everyone
else, they'd make fun of me, wouldn't I miss her and my sister?
Besides, she said, 'we don't need her charity, do we?' I told my
teacher we didn't take charity and I remember, even now, her sadness. I expect she'd seen a lot of kids like me go through her
classroom. Smart kids, kids who might have done something but
probably wouldn't.

In total we were in Hetton-le-Hole for around three years. I
had two best friends at school. Sonia, a giant of a girl who was also
a compulsive liar. We loved Hulk Hogan and kissed her poster of
him. My other friend was Stacey, whose dad was a policeman. My

mum always treated her with suspicion. I also had a brief best-friend flirtation with a religious girl until her parents met me and decided I wasn't the sort of child they wanted their daughter spending time with. There was a girl whose name I can't remember but whose mum was bewilderingly unkind to me. 'Sorry, Kerry, if I'd known you were coming I would have baked a cake,' she'd say with extreme sarcasm. Eventually she too told her daughter to stop playing with me.

On the estate I had a friend, a couple of years younger, who also had a single mum. Their house was nice, her mum did calisthenics, had a boyfriend with a fancy car and held Ann Summers parties. I tried to get Mum to be her friend, with my child's logic it made sense, but my mum mostly scorned her, maybe even hated her.

She did eventually make wary friends with someone who lived on our close. A glamorous woman, all shoulder pads and big eighties hair, who, my mum said, 'only wanted to talk about herself'. Downstairs was Ken, a tall, greying man who had furnished his flat entirely in brown. Thinking of it now, what comes to mind is a country and western lounge. When we first moved in he growled up at us and banged a broom handle at the noise we made but Mum went down and had a drink with him one night. After that he'd only do it sometimes.

Other things happened between the ages of eight and eleven but not many of them have stuck. I was in the local paper taste-testing ice cream and chose the cheapest one as my favourite. I got a place in the school brass band to play the French horn but I wanted to play the flute and so gave up. We acquired another cat that would jump up to the letter box to 'knock' when it wanted in. That little field with the swings that I walked through on my way to school was so peppered with dog shit that Mum just told me to walk through it even though my shoes were full of holes and held together with Blu-Tack. We all got terrible food poisoning from eating bad chicken – the sour stench of vomit wafted from the sofa and carpet for months afterwards.

Around this time my father started sending a little money for me but stopped abruptly when he found out Mum was spending it on all of us rather than just me (I'd told him my sister had got a tricycle). Still, each Sunday I walked down behind the pit cottages to the payphone outside the cricket club and made a reverse-charge call to him. Either Mum told me or perhaps I realised that good news should be my only news. No complaining, no telling tales.

At some point he came to visit for a few days, walking the streets of Hetton-le-Hole like a tourist in horror-fascination. He drank the whole time; so did Mum. I found them in bed together. He got into a fight in the local pub over the pronunciation of ballet (they were pronouncing the 't') and with my mum over the pronunciation of vermicelli (she was pronouncing it verma-*selli*). He left suddenly, still drunk.

This time is hard to order in my mind. I think of school as the good place and home as the bad place. Mum was particularly ill. She once sat down and told me that the sound of me chopping a tomato (I was making sandwiches for our lunch) made her want to scream. She drank a lot. She turned up late and drunk at the school gates (an uncomfortable thing to remember since that's what got me put into care that first time all those years before). Sometimes she didn't turn up at all. I'd come home, and she'd be sitting in her chair, my sister having wrought havoc – one day she'd even got into a giant tub of margarine. As usual, she'd be jolly when I first got home, happy for some company and entertainment, but once she realised I was upset – 'Mum, you're drunk!' – it would turn nasty and she'd be back to calling me names.

More and more I was not her child but her partner. I listened and shared her troubles, looked after my sister, took on her grudges with people, carried and lifted and comforted her. I constantly worried about us all.

I don't doubt Mum was struggling. She stopped speaking to Grandma for a while but Grandma liked the last word and eventually called the police, pretending there was a death in the family so they would track us down for her.

We didn't have a phone at that point, the connection charge was more than we could find, but soon enough we found the money somehow and Mum and Grandma spoke daily until Grandma asked for money for her electric bill which we sent (God knows where we found it) but then had to listen to her bragging about how good it was to have her wine and fags again. Even as a kid I could see that was fucked, literally money out of our mouths.

Mum continued her long sleeps; sometimes I would curl up with her too or I would watch my sister. Once I was nine, or maybe ten, Mum decided that I was old enough to look after my sister by myself. I learned to make us simple food, had phone numbers that I could use if needed, was told not to let strangers in.

Things did get better for a while. She went to the doctor. She joined Gingerbread, the charity for single parents, on the promise we might get a holiday away (we never did). She found a project for women in Sunderland where she was around people she liked and took classes there. She built a little bookcase she was rightly proud of, she suddenly had friends and started reading Germaine Greer. But once the project finished, she never kept up with any of the women. She enrolled in an Open University course in English, read Dickens and spent hours bent over in an armchair with a cheap notepad and biro trying to write her essays, but gave up after the first one saying her tutor 'didn't get it'.

I think of this period with a sense of happiness and foreboding. At some point during our time there Richie came back briefly, left us with nothing and ran away to a caravan in Hartlepool whereupon he and Mum reconciled, and we spent strange, cold weekends cramped in his caravan for my sister's sake.

At home, we didn't have visitors. My mum wouldn't allow my friends in the house. She went through long depressions, sitting in her dressing gown in her armchair by the fire, smoking endless roll-ups, talking down at me sitting cross-legged on the carpet. These would be endless monologues about 'them out there' and how I should be an 'iron fist in a velvet glove' – long, long lectures she called 'pep talks', her eyes too bright, her face unsmiling. 'Hey, Kerry, Kerry, come here. Come here, I need to give you a pep talk. It's up to me, I'm your mum, I need to protect you.'

When I was around ten I was diagnosed with genital warts. They were extreme and I had to attend the hospital several times to have them treated. I can't tell you how alarming this is if you are a young girl and there is a grown man doing that treatment. Though Mum was there in the room too.

HPV is known as an indicator of sexual abuse and certainly something changed in my sexuality that year. Perhaps it was simply my time to start becoming a woman, to begin my exploration of sexuality. I've often feared it was something else though. I cannot explain this fear beyond the idea that it is something that has lived with me for almost three decades.

I have thought about all the other possible explanations. That same year I went with friends to watch a film at a man's house who I later found out had been accused of paedophilia. I was taken by two friends who said you could go round to his house and he'd give you sweets and drinks and you could watch a film. I can't remember what happened in the end, I think perhaps Mum went round and told him to stay away. But perhaps he was simply a lonely older man who liked the company of children.

Around the same time, on the dirt path from the fields at the back of the house that led to school, I found, a few times, torn-out pictures from hardcore porn magazines, women with their legs open, vaginas splayed.

One day a man appeared. I remember picking up the picture, staring at it and him emerging from the field, my screaming and running away to school, terror in my wee heart.

Not long after this I called up sex lines from the newspaper with a friend and, putting on a deep voice to choose the story scenario, listened to descriptions of all manner of sexual acts.

I was left alone too often. I was allowed to roam freely. I had a mother who would likely not have noticed the changes in me. I was very much in need of love and far too eager to do anything at all for it.

I was given no indication or warning that I was, in fact, still a child. I watched everything on television that my mum did, much of it extremely sexually explicit. I was treated as an equal adult. I was given no protection. The idea that I might be innocent and that that was something that should be shielded and incrementally reduced was never an option.

That was when I really began to be terrified of falling asleep. I'd try and stay awake as long as I could. I needed the light on. I got huge patches of psoriasis all over my body and scalp, as though the anxiety was starting to seep out of my pores.

That summer I took to playing the game 'the Germans are coming', where my sister and I would hide in the airing cupboard for hours theoretically hiding from Nazis who would take us away (it was the year of an Anne Frank TV adaptation). We would hold our breath, heart thumping, waiting for the bad men to come.

Later, in Scotland, when I was eleven or twelve, I became convinced the Ku Klux Klan would come for me. I spent my whole life fearing one bogeyman or another.

Social workers did come and investigate. The house was tidy, I was about to go ice-skating with friends. I sat and answered their questions happily enough. When they were gone Mum was celebratory in the way a person would be if they'd won the pools. She congratulated me on my 'good answers'.

I understand this was a triumph over her long-term adversaries in the social services. And she felt satisfied she'd done her own checks. A few nights earlier, lying together on the couch, she'd asked me whether anyone had ever touched me. I said no, of course not.

I have known many people who have survived abuse and would not insult their bravery by claiming anything about my experiences. Perhaps they were just more symptoms of a chaotic childhood. I have to accept I'll never know.

Soon after the social workers' visit, Richie arrived bearing gifts. A pink ghetto blaster for me, an oversized cuddly toy for my sister. He had a new job, a good one. Two weeks after I had started high school my mum took us all up to North Lanarkshire in a National Express coach to live in his spare room.

17
Hetton-le-Hole
2018

The trip to Hetton-le-Hole didn't start normally. It started at an award ceremony in Newcastle where I was to present some writing prizes that I'd judged. It was in a beautiful building at the university, there was a seating plan as you entered, I think there were even fake trees.

When I walked in nervously I saw someone I knew a little who immediately and efficiently said, 'Who would you like to meet?' I'd only just learned that when people say this it isn't because they think you've come with a list for networking but instead because they are done talking to you and that's the politest way to disentangle themselves. After wondering where people learn such things, I'd started answering, 'No one really. But don't worry, I can look after myself,' before wishing them a good evening, giving them a wide smile and a squeeze on the arm, which is what I was taught to do in my world when letting someone down gently.

The seating arrangement told me I was at the top table with another writer, the director of the organisation, a TV historian and lots of important older men.

I wasn't drinking because I was due to give my presentation later that evening. I'd squeezed myself into Spanx and I was incredibly hot. I sweated profusely and, though I was happy to celebrate the winning writers' night and be part of a good organisation doing good things, sitting at that table with all it suggested made me uneasy.

The historian and I started talking. He was also working

class and grew up in the region and we talked about this book, our childhoods. I'm incapable of small talk, I always have been. 'The thing is, I think if you're forced to change yourself to navigate a world that isn't yours . . . well, it can make you a bit fractured. Turn you a bit weird.'

We leaned towards each other and though he appeared incredibly at ease – indeed, he was the star turn at the table – I wondered if he would also rather be seated further back or not at a lavish dinner at all. He told me that when he was first invited out socially by his university professor, along with some other students, he didn't know what to say to him. In the academic setting he never faltered but outside he had no idea about 'soft power', he'd never been taught it.

I didn't tell him that I'd never heard that term until he said it. Instead I smiled. 'You excel at it now though, don't you?' He laughed. 'Yeah, now I love it.' Soft power. I thought of the way people so often seemed to be manoeuvring through the various rooms of life knowing dance steps that I was never given, coolly asking, 'Who would you like to meet?'

After the dinner one of the older men at the table I'd spoken to briefly but who I'd found out little about except that he felt the Labour Party in Liverpool were horribly corrupt, came up and said to me, 'Lovely to meet you. I feel like I've been in the presence of greatness.' He was obviously important and probably rich. The comment was clearly sarcastic, but I gave him a kiss on the cheek, laughed, patted his shoulder and said, 'All right, darling, take care of yourself,' just as I did to old codgers leaving the pub at night when I was a sixteen-year-old barmaid.

Soft power. I was grateful I had a name for that ambiguous, secret language. And grateful that perhaps my upbringing had given me another version of that myself.

I went back to the hotel where, for some unknown reason, I'd been given a suite almost the size of our flat in Liverpool. I got into bed and called Peter while eating complimentary ginger biscuits. I left in the morning with all the tea bags, coffee sachets and toiletries tucked into my rucksack and a few quid left for the cleaners on the bedside table. Knowing the cleaners would have done exactly the same in my position.

Like many of the towns I grew up in, which had seemed so isolated, so far from anything, Hetton-le-Hole is, in fact, only an hour's bus journey from Newcastle. I sat on the top deck of the bus, right at the front, my feet up on the ledge, and watched the small suburban houses, then smaller pit cottages, then motorway, then Washington Shopping Centre with its grim, cement facade, and finally Houghton-le-Spring with its minuscule high street comprising pound shops, pubs and over-decorated coffee shops. As we rounded the corner I spotted a six-foot, weather-worn furry bear strapped to a fence, its head hanging, fur mottled – not quite an 'abandon all hope . . .' sign but it felt close enough. A bit of bewildered rubbernecking revealed a smaller but no less abused bear strapped on top of a white transit van advertising beds and mattresses. The bus trundled down the empty high street. When I say empty I mean Apocalypse empty, bubonic plague empty, though it was midday during the week and surely there might have been pensioners at least?

It's a short hop from Houghton-le-Spring to Hetton-le-Hole. I used to do this journey on the bus the other way to ballet class. First with Mum and then, once I was ten, by myself to save the adult bus fare. About three months in I learned that one lesson a week didn't mean I would become a ballerina no matter how hard I practised. I was properly fucked off with that unfairness. I could be the best in that class but without money for lessons and outfits and travel to auditions that was that. I went home that night and cried to Mum for hours in a fury. Eventually even the few pounds a week got too much, and my mum told me to tell the teacher I wouldn't be coming back. The teacher offered to waive the fees and I told her we didn't take charity, what was the point of continuing anyway, and never went back.

As we came into Hetton-le-Hole, I saw the old library building. That library was the first place I ever truly learned to love books – not just the safety, warmth and comfort the library represented. Until then I read the same books as my three-year-old sister – big picture books with lift-up flaps and giant writing. I think everyone thought I was remedial but, in my mind, quantity was the thing – who else could say 'I read eight books this week'? But at that library I began reading for my age and then quickly sped right on to the adult novels. Going to that library once a week, carrying home those books, that access to other worlds where people behaved as you hoped they might, was one of the greatest gifts of my childhood. As were the kind librarians who, no matter how many times we returned books my sister had ripped up or scribbled in, always just said it didn't matter and let us withdraw the maximum number of books again.

Mum used that library to research her own health, and the law around rent and divorce when Richie wouldn't give her one. She ordered in books about my sudden onset of psoriasis, the red scaly gashes on my chest and up my knees, the helmet of it covering my scalp (resulting in agonising weekly treatment with hot oil and a nit comb). Sometimes she'd leave me there with my sister and go and do the shopping. That tiny old building, so much like a chapel, was a lifeline. Except when I went past on the bus it wasn't a library any more.

The main centre of Hetton-le-Hole has ten to fifteen shops in a small oval with streets spanning out from that like spider legs and a main road running through it. It was quiet. Not quiet for a town or quiet for a village but deathly quiet. Quieter than even Houghton-le-Spring, quiet like a morgue. The shops were open but there weren't any customers. It made me feel a little short of breath, that emptiness contrasting with the busy little street I'd known all those years ago.

More so than anywhere else, I felt like a giant in this little village as I walked behind the doctor's surgery where Mum had rows and I was examined and referred for my genital warts and an ear infection that the doctor said might have made me deaf had it gone untreated longer (I could momentarily smell the rotten oily seep of brown fluid down my neck and feel the numbing pain down my jaw), to the newly refurbished swimming pool – no longer the beautiful Victorian baths – where I finally learned to swim aged eleven and where, after school swimming lessons, I'd drink a plastic cup of Sprite with crushed ice from the vending machine, my cold hair full of chlorine and sticking to my cheeks and neck.

Inside I asked the receptionist where the library was. As I left, I told her, as I'd started to, sounding like a mad person bearing witness to a miracle only they can see, that I learned to swim in these baths. She smiled politely – how could she know that for over a decade I'd had not even the thinnest thread, no photos, no friends, no trips 'home', to connect me to the child I used to be? It often felt like I'd never been a child at all, that only these eighteen years of burdened adulthood existed.

Did the primary school still do free swimming lessons? I asked.

'Yes, each week. There's one on today. I learned here too.'

'That's a lovely thing. I'm so glad they still do that.'

'Yes –' she laughed a little, surprised – 'it really is lovely actually.'

The new library occupied a small space in a centre that reminded me of a well-kept DSS office. There was the standard glass-fronted reception, bright blue noticeboards with posters for apprenticeships, AA meetings and benefits advice sessions. There were maybe four bookshelves, mostly crime and romance, and a tiny children's area. The librarian looked up, startled, when I walked in. I whispered 'Hi', and she nodded in an amazed way, I assume to see someone in there, and then stuck her head below the counter again.

It took me less than two minutes to tour the whole library and read the noticeboards too. It was a place so still and vacant that even my soft steps muffled by the carpet felt transgressive, and as I walked into the bright sunshine outside I mourned the old library for the kids like me and my sister, the mums like my mum, and for the safe, warm space full of help that had become a hollow imitation of what it once was.

Back on the main stretch I went into a charity shop and on meeting the pale eyes of the old man behind the till briefly plummeted into chilled panic. I walked trailing my hands through polyester jumpers, stealing glances back at his pink jowls and big, hairy hands. I slowly browsed the bric-a-brac and chose two tiny Lego figures, a cowboy and an astronaut, to remember this moment, to take home a little piece of that place and all it meant to me, good and bad.

I paid with adrenaline fizzing through my arms, though there was absolutely nothing to be afraid of. He was just a pensioner volunteering in a dusty charity shop who looked very unsure of himself in the face of a tall, grown woman with an accent he couldn't place.

*

I knew the way home. I remembered only too well the endless walk from our housing association estate to the town come rain or shine – though mostly rain. We never caught the bus except maybe when it was a Monday and there was shopping to bring home. Of course, it wasn't endless at all and in fifteen minutes I'd walked by the hairdresser's where I'd had a pixie cut aged ten and the old newsagent's where Mum had bought me sweeties in consolation for 'looking like a boy' – both somehow still doing business – and reached my primary school.

The school sat in one of Hetton's dips between two hills. Next to it was still the pub where Mum once took me, collecting me early from school for a 'family emergency', only to sit on the mouldy picnic benches out back and have egg mayonnaise (a boiled egg with salad cream glopped on, and honestly one of my happiest food memories) and a small, icy bottle of Coke while she drank beer and laughed loudly with a new female friend who I don't think I ever saw again.

I made a promise that I'd go there for lunch. That I'd go in and order whatever I wanted from the menu. But then I was distracted by the school.

My mum hated Hetton Lyons Primary and its endless events that required parental interaction and attendance: Christmas fair, maypole dancing, Easter egg and bonnet decorating, brass band performances, school plays, book fairs – the list was endless. Plus, the teachers were what Mum called 'sticky beaks'. They often gently enquired how things were at home. Mr Green offered me the pick of the good jobs: book fair monitor (you got to pick a free book so I picked the most expensive, a beautiful pop-up book, which just made sense to me) and 'projector girl' (which involved sliding a ruler down the acetate of that morning's hymns while they were projected on a screen to sing from – every morning I picked 'Amazing Grace' and 'Lord of the Dance' and everyone started to get a bit impatient).

Even standing on its threshold I felt a sense of belonging, of order. That school, those daft activities, the dedication and quiet care of the teachers, was one of the nicest things that ever happened during my childhood.

I hadn't set up any sort of meeting. I'd stopped doing that when the trips home started to feel overwhelming, deciding, instead, just to chat to people as I met them and follow up with telephone interviews. I wasn't dressed for it either, wearing candy-pink trainers and socks, cropped trousers, a red striped T-shirt. The outfit was designed for a day of walking comfortably, but it did give me a slightly eccentric look – part children's entertainer, part Dalston barista/VJ.

I am not a brave person. I am scared of strangers for all sorts of reasons. I've learned, when absolutely forced, to appear confident. I like to chat to strangers but I will move heaven and earth to avoid interactions where I might be judged. (How strange, then, that I've ended up writing my whole life down here.)

Despite my nerves, I walked into the school. Curiosity and attachment are strong instincts in me. Stronger than my social anxiety or fear of judgement, perhaps.

I remembered a school of lino, dark wood, mops and buckets in the corridors, but this was modern. There were big glass doors to access the school and an impressively large reception. The woman behind it was in her mid-twenties, smiling, her accent grown in that region if not in that very village.

'Can I help you?'

'Oh, hi, yes I . . .' I wanted to feel the comfort of walking through these doors again? I'm engaging in a strange personal experiment and this is one of the greatest hits on the route? I'm looking for all the things I lost, or abandoned, over the last twenty years, can you help with that? 'I'm sorry just to drop in. I used to go here around 1989 and 1990 and I was just curious. Have you refurbished?'

Her expression was polite but closed off.

'We did.'

'You know, I was only at this school for two years but it was the best one I was ever at.'

Her face opened a little; she tilted her head in a motherly way though she was at least a decade younger than me. 'I'm trying to think if there's anyone still here from that time.'

'Mrs Stafford? Mrs McClaren? The head teacher was Mr Green, he was such a good head teacher.'

'Doug? Doug Green. He's still working. I mean he's retired but he's a trainer now. I did some training with him a few months ago.'

'My God! Do you have his contact details? Or, no, sorry, maybe I could leave mine? I'd just really like to say thank you. I understand safeguarding and things, I know it's not possible to look around. My childhood was –' what word would I use? – 'difficult. But Mr Green, this school, was so encouraging. I'm a published novelist now and . . .' She looked at me, impressed or perhaps just endeared by this stranger coming in off the street telling her their life story on an average Friday afternoon. I blushed. 'I could never have done it if it hadn't been for this school. It was really special.'

Something clicked, as though she'd decided something, and she nodded.

'You know what. I'll see if the deputy head is around and she can talk to you more. Maybe introduce you to Mrs Smith who might have been here when you were.'

And with the efficient bustle of a woman who meant

business she strode from behind the desk and through the giant glass doors letting in a strain of childish noise.

The deputy head was a glamorous, very professional woman, and I was embarrassed anew to be dressed like a scruffy gondolier. She led me into her office and I explained about the book, about my connection to the school.

'I'll actually be seeing Mrs Stafford tomorrow for a reunion.'

'Really? Ah, it's a shame I'm not in town for longer. Would you pass on my regards? I'm sure she won't remember me but she was so kind.'

Mrs Stafford drove a jeep and wore tan 1970s knee-high boots and only drank Horlicks (which when I was nine seemed like the height of sophistication and I vowed that would be all I'd drink when I was grown up too).

I asked her if the area was still deprived and she told me it was.

'You know, of all the schools I went to this was the one where the teachers tried not to make me embarrassed about being poor.'

'I'm glad to hear that. We've actually just been through poverty proofing.'

She explained poverty proofing had been set up by the charity Children North East and began in 2011 when disposable cameras were given to children across the region who were asked to take photos of what poverty looked like in their local area. Nearly 11,000 photographs were returned. With them, the young people who took the photos communicated that the place where they found it most difficult to be poor was at school. Children North East then started 'auditing' schools, like Hetton Lyons, and were able to establish which parts of the school day were especially difficult for children from poor backgrounds in order to 'poverty proof the school day'.

The things that were difficult for low-income kids included being identifiable as receiving free school meals, being told off for not having resources or the correct uniform, missing out on trips because of the cost, missing out on PE because of a lack of PE kit, feeling left out during show-and-tell time, being bullied for not having the same branded clothing, phones or accessories as their peers, not being able to access extra-curricular opportunities because of the cost of public transport if they missed the school bus.

The charity concluded that schools should try to imagine the school day through the eyes of their poorest child and take this into account before undertaking any event or activity.

The deputy head told me that one of the biggest problems they discovered during their audit was water bottles. Parents with limited means couldn't buy their kid the latest, expensive water bottle and other kids were quick to pick up on the haves and have-nots. I thought of my little navy knitted 'uniform' and all the kids telling me I smelled and told her I understood exactly what that felt like. They solved the problem by introducing an affordable standard, school-branded water bottle and that small amount of sensitivity made some kids' lives easier.

'Would you like to look around?'

'If you've the time I'd be so grateful.'

The school was beautiful. We walked through corridors full of pictures, cheerful noises overlapping from the classrooms. Everything, even the cookers in their kitchen, was child-size and I had the feeling once again of being a giant. She told me they had a breakfast club and an after-school club to help working parents. That school trips are free and everything is as inclusive as possible.

'When I was here the town was . . .' on the bones of its arse, 'really struggling.'

She nodded, spoke a little lower as we walked out into the playground where I once made up routines to *Grease*. 'Yes, it's still in the 20% of the most deprived but all the parents get involved. Whatever we're doing. The biggest problem we have is drugs . . . they target them, the young vulnerable mothers.'

'My God, that's awful.'

For a moment she looked less glamorous and much more like a woman with the weight of the lives of hundreds of kids on her shoulders. I tried to imagine knowing you're sending home a kid to an unstable, potentially unsafe house. Their little limbs and hope-ful, daft ways. Their innocence and trust. 'You guys do amazing work. I could never do what you do.'

Back inside we passed a music class with its jangle of tambour-ines and shriek of recorders.

'I'll take you to meet Mrs Smith. She might remember you.'

I shook hands with a younger teacher and then with Mrs Smith who had worked at the school for forty years. She was slight, her hair, face and pink jumper all unnaturally pale in the primary colours of the corridor. It made me tender for her.

'I don't think you were my teacher – I would have remem-bered. But it's wonderful to meet you.'

'I probably taught you country dancing.'

'Yes! Thanks to you I can still hold my own at a ceilidh!'

'And brass band.'

'Oh, I was the worst band member ever. I got French horn but would never practise. I used to watch the other kids' fingers instead of reading the music.' I thought I saw a shadow of disapproval and tried to make amends. 'I'm a novelist now. I'm published by Penguin Random House. I've written two of them. This will be my third book.'

Her eyes widened. 'Very good for you. Congratulations.'

Like getting a gold star. I couldn't have been more bashfully proud if I was showing her a picture of a dragon I'd just painted and scattered with glitter. I looked at my shoes. 'I couldn't have done it without this school. You know, I think the teachers knew things weren't good at home and . . . they looked out for me. Mrs McClaren offered my mum her daughter's clothes for me and my sister, Mrs Stafford found a way to offer the camping trip to me when we couldn't afford it.'

'I'm glad. I'm glad about that.'

Somehow, I ended up holding hands with this woman I'd just met in that hot little corridor with its soundtrack of recorders and tambourines. I held her small, weightless hand and we were both teary. 'Sorry, it's really emotional being back. Thank you so much. Really.'

We hugged, said our goodbyes, I promised to send her my books.

I thanked everyone again as I left, took down the names to send the books to and waved goodbye.

Outside I turned right onto the hill that would take me to my old house. It was sunny and warm and I walked smiling as I climbed. Past the old folks' home where I used to go and ask if I could 'volunteer' to talk to the old folks though none of them wanted to be bothered by me really, up by the cricket club where I sometimes spent my pocket money on a pineapple juice, and the phone box, just a patch of concrete now, where I'd wait for my dad to call (or not) on Sunday afternoons, or I'd reverse charge until we realised how expensive those calls were. Up the back lane behind the pit cottages with decaying wooden gates and crumbling red brick. So little had changed. Even me, still touched and warmed by the kindness and interest of good teachers in a good school doing their very best against all the challenges that town presented them with.

*

In order to get to the semicircles of red-brick houses that made up my old housing estate I took a short cut. A little dirt path riven by footfall over decades, between a field and some allotments. The same path where I'd once found the porn and that old man had found me staring at it and I got the fright of my life. It was clear I should never have walked that path alone, not at nine or ten years old. Even as an adult in the sunshine, with the yellow tall grass swaying one side and the allotments spilling their bright wild flowers through the chain-link fence on the other, I felt a subtle sense of alarm, the same one that all women learn on quiet, out-of-the-way roads, in places where they might be pulled away, chased, touched, brushed against. Just a slight tensing of the senses and muscles no matter how bright the day or how short that quiet road.

But once I emerged I was amazed by how pretty it was. A huge field – straight green horizon as far as the eye could see – and fat-bellied old horses grazing away within it just as they had when I was a kid. Like I'd never left, there they were waiting for me to feed them Polo mints from an exaggeratedly flat palm already covered in the sticky residue of horse saliva.

The swings were gone but still, I thought, what a picturesque place to live. All this space, your own personal horses. I remembered how, in the field with the tall grass, I'd trap moths, letting them flicker in my cupped hands to catch the bronze shimmer from their wings. How I'd play with my friends on all these streets and walk with my sister to the nearby man-made ponds and dig for frogs the size of pebbles in the warm mud. I was eleven when we left – probably exactly the age when I would have begun to feel the sting of the town's harsh limitations – but, for a while, as well as everything else, there were happy moments of a proper childhood that I'd almost entirely forgotten. Yes, I thought, you really do always feel the slaps harder than the strokes.

The whole estate, in keeping with the theme of the place, was deathly still, absolutely silent, even the breeze seemed to ruffle nothing. When I turned onto the little close of four houses of flats that had made up our small crescent there was a couple sitting outside in the tiny communal area of grey paving stones. They sat on kitchen chairs, him with his big middle-aged naked torso browning darker under the sun and her, slim, small and in her fifties, still wearing a cardigan, her legs crossed, one foot twisted around the chair leg. As tightly coiled as possible, in contrast to his luxuriant stretch. Between them was a big bottle of orangeade and they both had fags on the go. It looked cosy, intimate even, and I felt guilty for intruding. But in an estate where there seemed to be not another soul it was never going to be an option to not stop and explain why I was prowling around.

'I used to live there.'

I pointed behind them to the window that had been my room. They were suspicious – my clothes, my seemingly aimless wandering, my eager smile. He was a little friendlier than her. 'That's where she lives now.'

And the luck, the coincidence, made me laugh. 'My God. Really?'

She looked even less impressed because, of course, it wasn't so surprising to her that she'd be sitting outside her own flat.

'Yeah, five years I've lived here now.'

'Would you mind if I took a few pictures of the outside? Just for memory's sake?'

I felt that she wanted to refuse me, but also once I'd voiced it I couldn't take it back without digging into why she wouldn't want me to. Besides, I still felt it was my house, I had been there first, and why shouldn't I have the right to take a picture? Though it wasn't my house any more and I didn't have the right at all. The man leaned back a little more and swigged some of the pop. Not his circus, not his monkeys.

'Are you sure it's OK?'

'All right.'

I took a couple and walked back to them.

'Thanks very much. Do you mind me asking how the estate is now? Is it a nice place to live?'

She shrugged and took a puff on her cigarette. 'They gave us new doors.'

The man sprang upright, laughing. 'New doors but the insides is a state, mind.'

I laughed along with them and then asked, 'Is it still a housing association? Do they do enough? Keep it safe enough?'

The woman looked at him and then at me. 'You're not from them, are you?'

The man spoke up: 'Spying!'

And I laughed again, trying to put them at ease. 'No, I'm just revisiting my old haunts. For research. I'm a writer.' I knew, in fact, that wouldn't put them at ease at all but it seemed wrong to lie, even by omission.

For a moment I thought she might offer me a look inside my old house. I could see that if I asked, with even just a little assertiveness, she would let me, despite not wanting to. And I very much wanted to see it. But she looked, as the women in my family would say, like 'she lives on nerves and fags' and I didn't want to put her out at all. 'Well, thank you so much. For letting me take the pictures. It was lovely to see it.'

As I turned to leave she shouted after me.

'You could try talking to Pam over at 72 – they've been here for years.'

'OK, thank you. Enjoy the sun!'

Before I'd even stopped speaking they'd closed their eyes and tilted their faces to the sky again and I was glad they looked so happy.

I didn't go to see Pam. I knew I should. If I was being a good writer and researcher, then I would, but I didn't want to interrupt someone else's summer afternoon. Let Pam do what she was doing. Besides, I felt for the first time properly that I was doing what I was meant to too.

I walked up through the rest of the estate. It was even shabbier than I remembered it, though still nicer than most of the places we lived in. I decided to walk up the hill to the little straggle of shops where we'd sometimes go for groceries. I remember, my stomach plunging in shame, that I used to call one of them Paki Paul's. Everyone I knew did and though Mum was vehemently anti-racist she let it slide too. She also trained me to say, when I went in with paper money, 'That's a five-pounds,' as I handed it over in case he short-changed me. Though he never had. She'd often send me with a handwritten note for tobacco and drink, as parents did then, the flourish of her biro signature at the bottom.

When my dad came and heard me use that expression he was horrified and tried to explain to me repeatedly why I shouldn't say it.

'But that's what it's called, Dad,' I insisted, exasperated with his southern insolence. 'That's the shop's name.'

'That's not the shop's name, Kerry.'

He was drunk as usual but he was still lucid and I'm glad he did get me to stop saying it.

I passed a house on the corner where an old friend used to live. A nice two-up two-down. She had a big bedroom with posters, toys and make-up, and one summer we sat on the bed in our swimsuits and listened repeatedly to *Now That's What I Call Music: 17*. That's also where a Dobermann, who was always very interested in my crotch, bit my arm and I ran all the way home in my swimming costume, bawling my eyes out, though he hadn't even broken the skin.

I was shocked by the absolute lack of change in every place I'd revisited. But no more so than in Hetton-le-Hole. Almost three decades had passed and everything was the same. There was the same dentist where I got eight fillings all in one go. There was the church hall where I went to a Halloween party dressed as an astronaut with a foil-covered cardboard box as my helmet. There was the shop where my dad took me to buy a tub of Neapolitan ice cream each night of his visit – an extravagance that made me believe he was rich.

As I approached I saw one of the windows of the shop had been smashed, the sparkling fragments held together by a large window sticker and brown parcel tape. Whenever I see a shattered window I always have the urge to finish the job, to kick the window fully in and see the pieces skitter. I'm not surprised that people who're feeling fucked off do that. It must, for a few seconds, be so satisfying – especially if you've nothing to lose.

I walked inside. It was just as I remembered – tattered lino, dusty tins and jars on shelves, a drinks fridge humming away and the post office in the back. There used to be metal bars across the top of the ice-cream fridge by the door in those days and cages on the fag display. Those were gone, so some things had changed. The thought came to me that I could afford anything here. If I wanted to, I could get a basket and fill it up to the brim and pay with a beep of my card (though it was in fact overdrawn at that precise moment) and it wouldn't be a big deal at all. I took my time walking around, settling into the feeling of being a grown-up now. The thought that I could buy fags or booze made me laugh.

I took my can of lemonade and bag of pickled onion Space Raiders to the counter and asked the South Asian couple how long they'd owned the shop. 'I used to come here, as a little girl.'

The woman was stunning; she looked down at my crisps and pop, and offered a wide, amused smile. I felt shy, the way I always do with beautiful people, and wanted to explain those were just what I fancied right then. I could see how it looked, a middle-aged woman chasing old memories. How it probably was.

Her husband tilted his head back and ran through the business owners, his cousin twenty years ago, they'd been there for ten. An older woman with soft white blonde spikes of hair and a denim jacket queuing behind me was pulled into the conversation. She said she could remember the shop back then but not who owned it. For a moment we were all talking dates, years and owners like colleagues solving a tricky problem. Then I beeped my debit card on the reader and said thank you, the woman asked for some cigarettes in an efficient way, everything was business again and we were strangers.

Outside I sat on a low wall in front of a small, neglected memorial and ate my crisps looking at a rough-looking pub called the Pit Lad that had all its windows frosted out. I felt instinctively it wasn't a pub I should go in and that it would be good material if I did. But I'd seen enough. I wanted to leave Hetton-le-Hole with the warmth of the sun and that nice moment in the shop as my final memory.

18
North Shields
2018

It was due diligence really. That morning I'd left my Airbnb in Gateshead and, unsure of what to do next, decided I might as well see how North Shields had borne up. I caught the metro and, when it stopped at Tynemouth for Whitley Bay, I said, 'Whitley Bay!' so much like an excited kid that even the dour-faced skinhead next to me had to crack a smile.

Of all the places we lived in, North Shields, our brief home before Hetton-le-Hole, is the one I have the fewest memories of. What I remember are our makeshift B&B dinners, the doctor's surgery when they learned, aged eight, I hadn't had any of my vaccinations, dancing to *Footloose*, hanging and spinning from the metal bunk bed. But the town I remember nothing of and I suspect that's because we rarely left our little room except for trips to the park or the supermarket.

The North Shields high street is of the kind that TV news rolls out when they want to talk about The Death of the High Street. There were nail bars, pound shops and lots of charity shops. There was the occasional little independent cafe or shop, but they looked empty and unloved, like a very dressed-up woman sitting alone in a shitty bar. I imagined that all but the most cash-strapped or location-bound go to Sunderland, the Metrocentre or Newcastle to shop. But there was something painful about seeing a town gutted of its centre.

The busiest shop by far was a charity shop stuffed full of rails and rails of clothes, everything for £2. I went in for a rummage. I'm so stingy in my shopping habits that if you compliment me on an item of clothing I can tell you the exact cost, no matter how old – a bargain-basement Rain Man. But this was mostly the sort that wouldn't make it to a 'proper' charity shop. I felt sad watching the other women root through the holey jumpers and snagged polyester dresses with their faces full of concentration and then guilty with the luxury of being able to leave because it wasn't what I'd choose to wear. Because, of course, choosing is the thing.

Standing outside Poundstretcher I tried to orientate myself. I spun round in a circle. I did, I thought, have a vague recollection of the street. Like when you smell something but the attached memory is just out of reach. I tried to relax. Nothing on the agenda today, I told myself. I started walking. The streets were neat and mostly fairly attractive. There were nice houses and decent cars. A few large older buildings which were nice on the outside but – I could tell just from the drooping curtains and shabby nets – inside were less than lovely flats. Funny, the things we learn. I can deconstruct an area after only a few minutes: how safe it is, how rich or poor, if it's a good place to bring up kids. The hints are mainly subconscious. I just know, and I've never been wrong.

I walked on autopilot and stopped to watch a sack race at a school sports day. I laughed and rolled my eyes along with a harassed dad who'd only just arrived, out of breath and holding little trainers aloft like a prize cup. I knew the other adults thought I was a parent and felt marginally fraudulent but standing there also made me think about the possibility of that future and so I stayed a little longer.

'Remothering' someone once called caring for a child when you're an adult who's experienced a difficult childhood. You learn what parental love is through giving it to your own child. It sounded like a very risky experiment to me. How could I know I'd be strong enough to change a cycle centuries old? Still, I watched until the end of the race, cheered and clapped with all the proud parents and then drifted away to call Peter, just to hear his voice.

As we talked about nothing at all I meandered.

'Hold on, can I call you back? I think I've just found something.'

A round silver plaque said that the 'Development of Housing for Rent was opened on the 15th October 1990'. The last time I saw that building I was watching from our room over the road while it shrieked flames at the sky and the roof beams collapsed in on themselves.

And there, to my right, was my old school with its sports field where I learned to bowl a cricket ball and the park with the diagonal path that I walked from the B&B to the front gates. I stood at the gates and stared into the school. A woman waved as she left in a four-by-four obviously assuming I should be there, maybe that I was a parent, and I waved back but then retreated, embarrassed.

I walked my old route through the park. I remembered begging to play there after school, saying Mum could watch me from the window, but instead I was always to be home, inside that little room watching TV or reading hunched up in my bunk bed.

Even as I stood outside the building I wasn't sure. The architecture was right, the positioning. It still had the same, almost Gothic, exterior. But it looked . . . posh. There was a Farrow & Ball-esque shade of gloss on the front door and two neat topiary bushes in cream pots. I walked to the back and saw a shiny, white Mini Cooper parked up. Maybe they'd converted the big old house into luxury flats. Or maybe the B&B had just had a makeover the same as me – perhaps the insides were the same but the outside had had some upgrades.

A man came out the back door. He was maybe fifty with

sunglasses perched on his head. I felt like I'd been caught spying but then I noticed his giveaway green lanyard dangling from his neck and relaxed.

'Can you tell me, in the late eighties, was this a homeless hostel?'

He confirmed it was and I climbed the steps to meet him at the door.

'My name's Kerry Hudson. I used to live here then. The top room with the little windows in the roof? I'm a writer now. I'm writing about it.'

I shook his hand with a businesslike confidence I didn't feel. I've always had the sense that something is being ripped raw when I expose myself in this way, that I'm not a professional thirty-eight-year-old at all but a former homeless kid. Someone who lived in a single room with her mother and sister. I noticed the usual change in him, the more careful assessment of me and who I might be now, but it was soft, kind.

Kevin turned out to be a case worker at the house that was now a hostel for people with mental health issues. He told me when their organisation took it over they gutted the whole place.

'It must have been pretty rough back then.'

'We had a little fridge and a hotplate in the room to do our cooking. 20p for a shower.'

He looked bewildered by the idea. 'You're obviously doing well. And your mum and sister?'

'My sister's OK. She trained as a nurse.'

I took the name and contact details of his colleague, Kath, who was there when they took over the building. Later that day he'd follow me on Twitter and tell me he was looking forward to the book.

I walked away happy. There was something liberating in

hearing him confirm that house had been a rough place because, of course, I always knew that really. That we should never have been there in the first place.

Somehow, meeting him outside that B&B made me feel more complete. Seeing the place, standing there as a grown woman, meant that I didn't need to hold on to those feelings any more.

On the metro back, I decided to get off at Whitley Bay. I bought chips and curry sauce and ate them on a bench overlooking the sea, my hair tumbling into my face, the wind flapping through my clothes.

In front of me, two blonde sisters played in matching blue and pink dresses. The older sister, maybe five, kept moving away and her little sister came toddling after her. The older one took a few more steps, the little one staggering after her, an adoring smile on her face. Eventually the older sister picked the tot up by the waist and carried her back to their parents' blanket where the whole cycle began again. I laughed and laughed as I watched them.

I will always be sad for the loss of a lot of things but that day I also felt so grateful. Grateful that I was slowly getting to stitch the scattered parts of myself together again. Sitting there, eating my chips on that freezing beach, I almost began to feel like a real person.

19
Coatbridge
1991

When Mum told me we were moving to Scotland again I didn't realise we were moving to Coatbridge, a town along from Airdrie. But I do think I tried to reason with her that maybe moving in with Richie wasn't something that ever went well.

There are a few plausible explanations for that strange and sudden move from Hetton, which was our longest time living anywhere. Richie arrived with money and promises of finally having a job, and Mum was bored and lonely and far too optimistic. I also suspect she felt trapped by the idea of spending another five years in Hetton-le-Hole and thought it was better to pull me out of secondary school sooner rather than later. I think anywhere was better than wherever we were as far as she was concerned.

We moved into Richie's council flat several floors up a tower block in one of Scotland's most deprived estates. Richie's flats were always clean but sparse (the ex-soldier in him, I guess). They smelled of roll-ups and farts because the only meal he ate was eggs, chips and beans. There would be all sorts of little shelves put up holding jam jars of nails and screws. Miraculously, there was a little black-and-white TV with a knob to turn to get reception. In the spare bedroom where my sister and I would sleep there was a single bed which he'd found out on the street or in a skip and we would wake up covered in the pink welts of insect bites, exhausted, blood under our fingernails from scratching at night.

Having come from provincial little Hetton-le-Hole with its red-brick houses, walled-in gardens and fields with ponies, the estate itself was terrifying. Like the places poor people had to live in in futuristic films about the end of the world, where cannibals roamed the streets in bike helmets, holding pickaxes.

When we got there Mum said, 'You said the place was all furnished.' Richie swept his arm over the near-empty living room, a table by the window, a plywood coffee table, a raggedy couch, and said, 'Aye.' In the first weeks there I spent much of my time trying to ignore Mum and Richie arguing. I was on a wordsearch jag and I lay on my stomach only occasionally standing to go and look outside at the expanse of grey, the huge looming buildings. I knew little of council estates, having left them when I was so small, but I didn't have to be old or wise to know it was a hostile environment.

The move, the coach tickets, the little snacks and expenses along the way had wiped us out for money and we lived on chips for weeks. On a rare excursion into the outside world I went to the local shop. There was that tiny shop, a bookmaker's and a Chinese takeaway next to a large scrub of green at the end of the estate, marking the boundary with another estate, Greenend. The scrub of green was always litter-strewn, sometimes there would be an abandoned car. The shop itself was a fortress of aluminium caging. To choose you had to push your nose to the wire and then say what you wanted through a little hatch. There was a sign that said, 'Please do not ask for credit under any circumstances.' My dad, who must have visited briefly though I don't remember it clearly, still spoke about that shop fifteen years later. 'That was real ghetto stuff,' he'd say, laughing, never stopping to consider that he'd simply left me there, that I used to go to that shop for my sweeties.

In our first week, after going to the shop, my mum and I had to run through the streets of the estate away from kids who were standing on the garage roofs throwing rocks down at our heads. Mum went back to the flat raging, demanding Richie do something, and so he slowly, moderately resentfully, put aside his paper and his roll-up and went out.

We stood behind him as he went from shouting 'Come on, we've all had our fun' to 'I'll punch yer teeth so far down your throat you'll have to shove yer hand up yer arse to bite yer nails' as the kids, unalarmed, continued throwing stones. It was probably the most attention they'd been paid in a long while.

Eventually Richie got sick of me being home all the time and told me to go out and play.

'But I don't have any friends.'

'You could make friends in borstal.'

'What's that?'

'Never mind. Out. I want you out for at least an hour.'

So, I put on my roller skates and crabbed my way awkwardly down the dark flights of stairs and wheeled back and forth over the ten metres of broken paving slabs outside our block until the hour was up.

It was less than a month before everything collapsed. My mum told us we were only stopping until we could get a flat of our own. All of our possessions and the TV were moved into our room and we slept, the three of us and Gracey the cat, in the flea-ridden single bed.

I know we stayed there long enough for me to start at a Catholic school (Richie's choice) with maroon blazers and a coach that stopped at the edge of the estate to pick us up, only to leave again for a secular school (Mum's choice) in town.

One night there was a row which began with Mum and Richie drinking in the kitchen, her storming upstairs and Richie storming after her, waking both me and my sister. Mum was screaming and Richie opened a window, picked up the little black-and-white TV and threw it out. It smashed several floors below. He was a big man and it was terrifying. Just like the thought of living without TV.

I was eleven going on twelve. I had the wrong accent – half Northumbria, half Aberdeen, posh apparently, though it wasn't. I had the wrong clothes. I had no friends, no family ties. Worse than all those things, though, I was clearly, visibly, the worst thing you could be – I was poor. It was inevitable that I'd be slaughtered at high school.

I was, in the truest sense of the term, a weird geek. I loved Meat Loaf and Bon Jovi. I read countless books and looked forward to my visits to the library more than anything. More problematic was the fact that I told this to anyone who would listen.

Basically, I'd never been taught to just shut the fuck up when my opinion was unpopular. Richie once gave me a sliver of good advice that might have made my early teens easier if I'd taken it: 'Just be quiet and watch what everyone is doing.' But I'd been raised to speak my mind, by someone who treated me like a peer and who felt we were better than most of the people we were forced to live alongside. No matter how obvious it was that, in fact, we were doing a lot worse than most of the families in our community.

In my first week at Coatbridge High School I turned up to PE in the kit that we'd bought for my other, now abandoned, school, in Hetton-le-Hole – navy gym pants, knee-high socks, tennis shirt – to the hilarity of the whole class. Later in the year I cried in the middle of English when I got a C. I invited a girl who had been tormenting me to fight and the whole year turned up to watch. But as soon as it started, the idea of actually hitting someone seemed unthinkable. I ended up lying in the dirt with my washed-out grey training bra on show. My trousers were always three inches too short. My shirts had yellow sweat stains. My mum cut my hair at home and it grew out, still does in fact, at strange angles.

I started a school newspaper but only wanted to write anti-racism articles. I'd just seen *Mississippi Burning* and had decided to be a civil rights officer when I grew up. The newspaper lasted one edition. In social sciences our teacher asked us to sit down if we thought Jamie Bulger's murderers deserved to receive the death sentence. I was the only one left standing. I looked around the room and declared to my fellow classmates, 'You're no better than murderers yourself then!' Though my politics were sound you can probably guess how that went down with a room of eleven-year-olds.

I can't imagine why I was bullied.

I can see how, in many ways, I made myself an irresistible target, but it's amazing how precise in their cruelty kids can be. I can see why teens are recruited for despotic regimes because they are already clever enough to perceive the most vulnerable parts of others but haven't matured enough to understand just how deep the damage they are able to inflict can be.

One day I sprained my ankle jumping down a step. While my classmates stood in line and laughed waiting for the teacher I begged one after another of them to go and get someone for me. When the teacher finally arrived he laughed right into my weeping face too, until, still rolling his eyes, he helped me to the school nurse.

I wasn't being dramatic, my ankle was black and blue and swollen up like a tennis ball. I've still never forgotten, not the pain, but my absolute despair that people could be so unkind.

School became not about learning but about hiding. Constantly toughening myself up against nasty words – you couldn't cry, no matter what – and small, petty acts of violence. Each morning I walked up the hill in anticipation of what hurt or shame that day might bring. Each afternoon I walked down it heady with relief I'd survived. Except for a few kind teachers (history, RE and art), I felt disliked by both staff and classmates.

I suspect my teachers didn't warm to me for a number of reasons: I wasn't local, I was vocal in my opinions which weren't always welcome (that social sciences teacher strongly believed in the death penalty), and I was poor. Perhaps they mistook trying to grapple with a new curriculum, a new school and the treatment I received every day for stupidity.

I was a kid who came to school loving books and learning, and with curiosity and an enthusiasm for what education could lead to, but they had drummed it out of me almost entirely by my second year with harsh words, impatience and sometimes outright hostility. I once came second in a gymnastics contest and the teacher, ignoring me standing in front of her, said to the winner, 'You almost let her win.' That 'her' came with a look of disgusted contempt. I didn't do any sport again until I was thirty.

A few weeks after I started that school, my mum finally got a council flat in Greenend. It was in a four-flat building at the end of a long road that curled right around the estate, which was made up of lines of once-desirable cream tenements, and which now stood in row after row of grubby blocks.

Greenend got its name from the scrub of grass next to it. Maybe there were bins burning on that green when we pushed along all of our belongings in stolen shopping trolleys, or maybe the smoking remnants of discontent and boredom is just what I conjure when I think of the place. Even Richie called it cowboy country.

It was true there was talk of people's houses being 'burnt out' if they pissed off the wrong folk. Even I felt, as we wheeled those trolleys towards our tiny flat, we could have been a bit more discreet, a little less brazen about announcing our arrival as fresh meat.

The flat was, like every council property, spartan and utilitarian to the point of comedy and we'd nothing to fill it with. There was the standard-issue worse-for-wear brown carpet, the usual empty rooms with cheap woodchip on the walls. My mum took yet another loan out from the social for second-hand furniture, white goods, plates and forks, a few pans and bedding, to be paid back bit by bit each week. The repayments weren't much at all, maybe a few pounds, but we always felt the absence of those few pounds come Sunday when the cupboards were bare and we were all starving hungry.

Our downstairs neighbour was called Claire, a single mum to her son Andrew, an eight-year-old with a tangle of blond hair who was obsessed by football. He played out front and me and my sister took the backyard with its twist of near-dead trees and damp laundry always flying in our faces. One day my sister, now three or four, found and took home a used syringe, like bringing home a prize. Then we didn't play there any more.

My dad disappeared for a while at this point. For a few months, maybe even five or six, he didn't call at all. Then I received a scrawled postcard. He'd been in Mexico, he'd been in Ireland. He'd had Bell's palsy. He was going back to London and I could visit him, or we could go on holiday together.

I believed him and took armfuls of travel brochures from kindly travel agents who must have known I wasn't going anywhere when I proudly declared 'my dad's taking me to Greece'. I pored over hotel rooms and all-you-could-eat buffets (all you could eat!) and beaches with white sand and aquamarine water, kids' clubs and swimming pools with slides. All while lying in front of our electric bar fire in my second-hand pink fleecy dressing gown reeking of my adolescent sweat and its previous owners. It won't surprise you to hear that looking at those brochures was the closest I ever got to those buffets and beaches with their rows of primary-coloured umbrellas.

Of all these memories, writing about this time makes me the saddest. Perhaps because I was getting old enough to understand. The slow, cold, seeping realisation had started that life was hard and would likely only get harder. I couldn't survive any more on the kindness of teachers or childish fantasy – though God knows, I tried the latter.

We were very lost as a family. My mum was entirely isolated, except for Richie who would come around hoping for a loan or sometimes a kiss and cuddle. Mum did have a drink one day with the neighbours, but she'd had a half-bottle of vodka before they even arrived and, in the end, fell over in front of them. She shouted at us as I tried to wrangle her to bed and then she fell asleep until the next day.

The only time her and Claire spoke beyond strained politeness was when two men wearing balaclavas and holding crowbars turned up at Claire's door and Mum and me went out in our nighties onto the landing and shouted down to see if she needed the police. She said she didn't, we went back inside and that was that.

We had found ourselves in a place where, yet again, we didn't fit. I couldn't get used to the violence of the town, the shouts seemingly from nothing and nowhere, 'Haw, hen, yeh want yer hole kicked?' or 'Gis a gobble!' Each time I opened my mouth I betrayed my difference.

We spent our weekends together at the local park, where my sister loved the butterfly house, or at Summerlee, which was a tiny museum devoted to 'Scottish industrial life'. Mum went from charity shop to charity shop, 'second-handers', and I waited outside with my heart hammering in case I was spotted by someone from school. Me and my sister wore strange outfits put together by Mum – orange waistcoats and yellow jumpsuits. We watched TV together in the evenings until I fell asleep in front of the screen. Each school lunch break I used 20p to call and check in on Mum. I minded my sister so often and with such harassed expertise that people mistook her for my child.

I did briefly make friends on the estate, two girls who moussed my hair and loaned me lip gloss before we stood about in parks glittering with broken glass. But Mum decided I shouldn't spend time with them any more because she never saw me.

I still trusted in everything my mum said. I wore the strange second-hand clothes she gave me, and if she wanted me home, I stayed home. Our relationship was extremely intense simply because she was all alone and I felt I was at odds with everything and everyone around me. I wasn't just her daughter – I was the only person she trusted in the world.

But I was twelve years old and I was deeply unhappy. I was drowning not waving and pulling her and my sister along behind me as I tried to swim towards adulthood.

Then I joined the church. I don't remember exactly how it happened. I had been friends with a skinny girl called Michelle. A kid with a neat home and a fearsomely strict dad who loved the seventies rock band Runrig, possibly more than his wife. Michelle had white socks as grey and trousers as outgrown as mine, and that was mostly what we had in common.

We were inseparable for a year, maybe two, not out of mutual affection but because we were safer in a pair and making the best of it. We made up innocent games, wandered around the town avoiding other teens, practised balancing on railings, occasionally went to the swimming baths with a few pounds in our fists and tightly rolled threadbare towels under our arms. That last flush of childhood.

But then Michelle's dad decided he wasn't keen on me and my big gob and lack of parental discipline, as though those things might be contagious, so Michelle drifted away and I was forced to find new pals.

I ended up spending lunchtimes in a deserted corner of the school with two girls called Linda and Deborah, swapping *Smash Hits* posters (their Keanu Reeves for my Take That). Then spending weekends and going along with them to their houses, and then, finally, going in the car with Linda, Linda's parents and Deborah to New Light Church, a newly built, squat red-brick building in a rough part of Motherwell.

The New Light Church was an evangelical church based on an American model. I started off in the youth group – Youth Alive, I think they called it. There were perhaps twenty of us and a group of adults, who must have been in their twenties, who were youth leaders. We talked a bit about religion, and the good heart and good student in me appreciated the principles of Christianity. The chaotic teen in desperate need of kindness and uncomplicated care appreciated everything else about that small safe space with its endless tea, biscuits, listening ears and earnest cuddles from platonically engaged adults.

Eventually I went to Sunday service. A big, light-filled room with three waves of seating pointed towards a large stage. On that stage there would be a band complete with electric guitar. On a projector there'd be the words to Christian rock songs against cloud and ocean backdrops – like Facebook inspirational quotes before Facebook. As the congregation sang, there'd be drums and tambourines, some would dance in the aisles and the rest of us would hold our palms to the sky, clap and sway.

During prayers the band would play a soft melody, and as the cries of 'Oh yes, Lord, fill me, Lord' rang through the church, so would the rhythmic incantations of people speaking in tongues. Then they would ask all those who wanted to repent to step forward. Many of the congregation would stand in front of the stage while the pastor prayed, the band played and churchgoers cried out in support of the shedding of their sins. Then, appointed men would start circling those who were standing. As the sinful spoke in tongues, the pastor's hand pressed to their forehead, their limbs folded in on themselves as if in slow motion, and they were 'filled with the spirit'. They'd be caught by the appointed men standing behind them and lowered gently onto the floor. Afterwards, they'd help each other stand and then return to their seats and we'd all get up and have orange squash and tea and biscuits and hug each other goodbye.

The first few times I watched all this with fascinated bewilderment but, eventually, I joined in. I clapped my hands and sang along with the band. Soon enough I was up at the front and, though I wasn't sure about whether or not I was being filled, there was something powerful and deeply comforting about begging to be saved, about weeping for all the things there were to weep for. There was, for someone who was rarely touched or cuddled ('Don't be such a sook'), the comfort of falling back into strong hands and being gently cradled down to the floor. And after all that, somehow feeling brand new and special and drinking some sweet orange squash and hugging everyone.

The nonsense sounds of speaking in tongues rolled out of my mouth like a child learning to form words. I never truly believed God was speaking through me, but I knew that's what was expected. For the first time in my life I had friends and a place to go to where I was welcome and adults who cared what happened to me. I understood there would be some sacrifices to stay part of this community and conformity was stitched into the deal. I considered it a leap of faith.

The church hadn't fully thought through the targeted saving of kids from the rough estates, the fact that we still went home to difficult streets, sometimes difficult homes, to few prospects and the general chaos of hormones and confusion that is your teens. But it gave me a ready-made gang of pals living much the same life as me.

Mum was furious about the church. She didn't want me religious. She didn't want me talking to other adults. She didn't want me to be out of the house evenings and weekends and away from her. But now I had found something important to me and a whole theology to use as ammunition. Even my mum couldn't come up with a good argument to stop me from going to a nice church group and soon enough she gave up bitterly and nearly completely. You want to be an adult? Fine.

I stopped going home and slept at one church friend's or another's. Initially, the agreement was that I'd keep 20p in my purse and call Mum from a payphone to tell her I wasn't going to come home, but within a few weeks Mum just assumed that if I wasn't home then I was staying with friends, or perhaps the phone had been cut off. I was thirteen and left to wander the streets of another town with my new friends.

I drank cider and Strawberry and Kiwi MD 20/20 with them on old bridges. We smoked dope in one of the older boy's houses sitting on mattresses on his floor. I had my first kiss in the church car park with a boy who said I'd kissed like a dog (which might well have been true, I remember having no idea when I should move my head) and graduated quickly to 'stuff' and then to sex, losing my virginity at fourteen while blind drunk to a handsome sixteen-year-old boy called Paul. He told me he'd wear a condom for me and he didn't do that for anyone else. It could have been worse, I suppose. It was such a quick acceleration I barely noticed it. Perhaps a year from my first proper taste of drink to drinking as much as I could find. From my first kiss to sleeping with any random lad. From going home each night and watching TV with Mum to wandering around Motherwell's council estates with spare pairs of knickers in my rucksack not knowing or caring where I'd sleep that night.

I begged my mum to let me change to Motherwell High where most of my church friends went. She agreed because she couldn't bear my constant crying and also because I think she knew herself how hard my current school had become for me. My new school was huge and, because my friends were older, they were in different classes to me. I remember being in an English lesson where a girl asked me 'what you done?' Then she reeled off a load of drugs she'd done. 'Do yeh do jellies?' I saw her a few weeks later clinging to a lamp post, her legs like jelly themselves, gurning away, completely high.

I kept getting sent out of class for one thing or another. Eventually – I can't remember why – I just stopped going. I'd go around to Kenny's house, an older guy from the church who lived with his ma, and watch MTV and eat cheese toasties with him. Or I'd go to a little wooded area and eat a packet of cheap biscuits while reading my books. Occasionally I'd chance the library, hoping I wouldn't get caught skiving.

At church, Paul, who we'd all smoked dope with, got a girl pregnant and was told to repent or be excommunicated. He refused to say he regretted his actions, or his child, and so was cast out. A few of us challenged the decision, and when we saw that, actually, forgiveness was very relative indeed, we slowly stopped going to church. But without the church there wasn't much that connected me to those people, and with drink and fucking lads and dope on tick from the local dealer comes friction.

I ended up very lonely, with no pals and no home I felt welcome in. No school to go back to and, I now knew, no real hope for any future of my own. My mum was sick again, one day she told me she'd asked for a sign (though she also told me vehemently she didn't believe in my God) that she should keep going and at that very moment she heard kids in the streets shouting up at a squirrel running along our roof. 'A squirrel! Can you believe it?!' Clearly thinking it was a positive sign from God.

At the end of a long and lonely summer term, trudging around alone or sometimes trying and failing to ingratiate myself back into my group of pals by drinking more and smoking more and 'getting off' with more guys, trying to add my value in the only way I understood it, Mum got a letter saying I hadn't been in school.

The letter came at the same time as Richie visited or sent a postcard or phoned to say he was living by the sea and there were loads of 'digs and jobs'.

And that was that.

20
Coatbridge
2018

On the morning I had a train booked to go up to North Lanark-shire, I got a message from my Glasgow Airbnb host saying I might want to 'check the trains because of the weather' and another from an old friend, Sally, who I was off to visit while returning to some of my old estates, warning me to 'bring lots of jumpers!' I peered out at the flat, wet grey of our first Liverpool winter and wondered what could be going on beyond this small, sea-facing city.

The train ride was beautiful, through industrial towns and rural countryside, the snow falling like a picture postcard. I laid my head against the window and looked out and felt a strange sort of stillness come over me. I was on the train now and whatever would happen would happen.

Sally had sent me an email months ago with the subject 'googling an old friend and what do you find?' and the first line 'Kerry bloody Hudson that's who!' Sally was one of my closest friends when I was fourteen and attended the New Light Church. She was a dreamy, sweet teen with skinny wrists and a curly mop of black hair that was always falling into her eyes. Hers was one of the houses I often stayed at. We always ate the same dinner – a shared box of Kraft Macaroni Cheese – sitting side by side on her bed. The first time I ever used make-up it was hers. She believed in ghosts but felt badly because it seemed unchristian, she smoked but held the fag daintily between her fingertips like a child pretending to smoke with a biro. I hadn't seen her for twenty-four years.

When I first got her email, I sent her a warm, effusive one in return telling her not to worry about an argument she wrote about (which I couldn't remember) – 'Anyhow, none of us did adolescence well ... what a terrible time ... thank god we made it out!' – that I was often up to Scotland or she could come and stay on my boat (which I never did buy in the end). Then, in the way I have with my past, I simply closed off and let her other emails slide. I quietly retreated and blamed busyness and falling in love.

When I started writing this book I contacted her again and asked her if she might let me come and talk to her when I was back. I didn't really expect to hear from her, I'd treated her badly, but she responded and said of course she'd love to. She was a social worker now, a single mother, a knitter, she wore wigs for a change at the weekend. Once she got pregnant she had returned to Wishaw near Motherwell. She said she'd be happy to meet me and that seemed like a good enough reason to finally haul myself onto a train.

I'd always thought the winters of my childhood were imagined. The numb hands and feet that would start prickling and itching once warmed, the feeling that the wind was full of ice and was slowly stripping the skin off your body. But as I lugged my bag through the glittering pavements of Glasgow, I realised I just hadn't been back for a very long time.

The next day the snowstorms were worse, the temperature even lower. I edged my way through the streets towards the metro station along with kids in school uniform on paths like ice rinks, all of us taking stiff, bow-legged steps like we'd simultaneously shat ourselves and slipped a disc. It occurred to me that even in the coldest weathers down south I'd never experienced this pavement ice, which my cramped muscles remembered so well from my childhood, as I skidded and dithered along. Local authorities probably figured no one had anywhere important to get to in poorer parts so it wouldn't matter if the whole place ground to a halt and pensioners shattered their hip bones.

My boots were already letting in icy water. I thought of my mum: one pair of socks, two plastic bags, another pair of socks and then on with the boots. A walk around the living room to make sure the rustling couldn't be heard. I stopped to watch a kid hacking at a puddle of ice with his heel – another echo.

I took the train to Motherwell to meet Sally. I sat and watched the small towns with names I vaguely remembered – Cambuslang, Uddingston, Bellshill – slip by with the dizzying, fear-tinged amazement that I'd become used to with each place I returned to. At the train station, Sally was waiting at the top of the concrete steps. I walked up, smiling, hugged her, her chin resting on my shoulder, and we were fourteen again.

'God, Kerry, you haven't changed at all.'

This was untrue. Months of anxiety eating and daytime sleeping had given me a figure like a doughy apple, and when Sally knew me I was skinny as a rake, all angst and skipped dinners so I could hang out with my pals.

'I was going to say exactly the same thing!'

That was true. In twenty-five years, over the course of many jobs, a baby, different cities and heartaches, she had barely changed. A few lines around her mouth and eyes, but barely perceptible. A greater confidence in the way she held her body. Her hands were still and by her sides now instead of perpetually fluttering about her hair and face but, really, she was still just Sally waiting for me at the top of the station steps, daydreaming until I said her name.

She'd offered to take me to see her office and then drop me off in Coatbridge. We passed the New Age Christian shop where we used to buy trinkets and a pub where we'd nervously let two much older men buy us halves of lager and put their arms around us. She told me about the people she still saw, they hadn't changed either it seemed. I almost looped my arm through hers just as we used to as teens before I realised it had been two decades and I should maybe buy the woman a half of lager first at least.

In the Motherwell social work offices, where Sally mentors troubled teens through secondary school and into further opportunities after they leave, she introduced me to her colleagues, all of whom managed various large projects and oversaw teams of other social workers. I found the sure way she spoke to them such a surprise. As, I suppose, me confidently shaking everyone's hands and telling them about my book and its intentions must have been to her.

I had always imagined social work as a chaotic job – papers everywhere, the telephones ringing off the hook – but the office was plushly silent, old-fashioned, incredibly tidy. Sally's boss was a large woman in her sixties, who had worked in social work for thirty-five years. Alongside her was a brunette, smiling woman and another with an assertive way about her.

While Sally made me a cup of tea I mentioned that I'd gone to school in Motherwell and asked about the changes they had seen in their years of service. They all agreed one of the biggest issues was homelessness.

'You look down any street now and there's homeless people and that wasn't the case, even going back ten years. But people aren't homeless because they haven't got a home, they're homeless because of mental health, because of substance abuse which links with suicide, and I don't think the public see that. I think they see them as not human.'

One of the women told me, proudly, she was the 'lead' on suicide prevention for men – in 2017 three times as many men as women committed suicide in Scotland and those figures have been strongly related to deprivation. She explained they were having to find new ways to talk to men about depression. That men don't want to talk to their doctor or a social worker. They're far more likely to open up to a hairdresser or a trainer at the gym so they're recruiting volunteers from the community to do that. 'We've done work with McDonald's, faith communities, work with Morrisons and Asda so that everyone is talking about suicide. And I don't know if you remember, we used to talk about cancer as "the big C". We would not talk about it, we'd whisper "she's got the big C", but we managed to overcome that and we need to do the same for suicide and for mental health.'

Sally had to make a call and they kindly kept me company, telling me how their services are being moved online. But what, I asked, happened if those people didn't have computer skills? If they didn't have access to the Internet or computers? I felt that maybe these were questions they were either tired of or that there was no good answer for, but they told me anyway about new 'hubs' being developed in partnership with GP surgeries where people could get online and how every library in Scotland had a computer. It seemed rude to challenge them, they were the experts and, more to the point, Sally's colleagues, so I didn't ask about the people who do not, or cannot, leave the house, who can't afford the bus fares to the library, about those who would find using a computer challenging in any public space or about the librarians who have to become pastoral carers and benefits advisers as well as skilled professionals.

Sally came back jangling her keys and packed up a few things to take to her next meeting. As we left I thanked her colleagues and wondered aloud what it would be like for me and my family if we were living there now and still struggling as we had.

'In some ways worse.'

'Different I would say.'

It was the oldest of them, Sally's boss, who'd been so reserved until that point, who spoke up then. 'I am glad we're in Scotland. You see the influence of the Tories and their cuts and their attitudes to those on benefits. But tolerance, the feeling we should be support-ing each other in the community, I think we still have that here.'

On the way out I told Sally that in my house I had been brought up to believe that social workers were do-gooders who were out to get you, to be treated with suspicion at best. Now I felt nothing but empathy and respect for the difficulty of these wom-en's work. I thought of how it would play on my mind and my conscience to see a mum at the supermarket obviously worrying about the cost of the shopping, or a kid with a too-flimsy coat on, and wondered what it took to get through not just a year of that work but decades.

It comforted me somewhat that people who clearly had kind, decent hearts, as well as sharp minds and experience, were doing their best in this new version of our country. A version of our country where those who have the least power are the most maligned. As a recent UN report on poverty in the UK outlined, those most severely affected by the last eight years of austerity have been women, children, those with disabilities, pensioners, asylum seekers and migrants, and those living in rural poverty. In short, all the people these women would be doing their best to reach, whatever the barriers.

I left the office feeling I'd just met superheroes, the kind that get all the bad press and the shitty jobs but keep on trying to save those who need saving anyway.

We arrived at the car park. 'This is a nice car!' I said, but what I meant was 'Shit, Sally. You're driving!'

We got in but before Sally could start the engine I reached over and touched her slim wrist. 'I owe you an apology.'

Sally's new sureness dropped for just a moment. 'Oh, no –'

'No, I do. You sent me those lovely emails and I didn't reply. I'm sorry, I'm just . . . I've issues about interacting with my past.'

'Well . . . you're here now.'

'It's really lovely to see you. Thanks for all your help.'

The roads were slippery, the banks high with grey, brown slush. Fat snowflakes battled the windscreen wipers. She dropped me in a Coatbridge I didn't recognise at all and we arranged to meet up the next day. I stood up to my ankles in snow and at the roundabout with cars slowly circling it, a McDonald's by a huge sign for a retail park with a Next and a Costa and a Tesco. The air was full of the hush that heavy snowfall brings. I said to myself, 'Here I am then,' and started trudging to the row of industrial-container-type buildings where Coatbridge Foodbank was located. Sally had said I might find it interesting.

It was actually very nice just inside the door, like a small accountant's office, with a neatly carpeted reception area and a side room. Beyond that was the donation area with shelves and shelves of non-perishables. I explained myself in a bit of a garble, that I didn't want to interrupt their work, that I'd lived here, that I was writing this book and was hoping for a few minutes of their time, and was ushered in by Angela, a small woman in a blue fleece and pink wellies. She offered me tea and invited me to sit up alongside her on a desk in front of the shelves while the other volunteers crowded around us. It seemed everyone was keen for a chatter. I smiled and told them I spent my teens in Greenend. And just like that everyone relaxed. Even with my nice boots and coat and my polite way about me they knew what growing up in Greenend meant. It was a statement I'd use again and again with strangers over the coming days – 'See? I'm only here to tell my own story.'

They told me about the recent break-in they'd had, how the whole community had turned up to help donate more stock. They talked over each other, all keen to tell me how good people had been in the aftermath.

'It was like a tsunami after it.'

'Honest, it was tremendous.'

'It was everyone – businesses, locals.'

I shook my head for a minute, wondering who would ever steal from a foodbank. How hurt, angry, and potentially hungry, you would have to be to take food out of the mouths of people who are quite literally starving.

'We had one of them shoogly charity tins. You know, a donation one. They bashed that open. But there was just pennies in it.'

I told them how we were often short of food when I was growing up but that I didn't remember there being foodbanks. It seems frightening that there are so many now.

'Just now it's the benefits sanctions that's really hitting people. And that's through no fault of their own. We even get people in here who have a job but they're not getting paid for a month.'

'Plus, people are working but they're not getting fixed-term contracts or holiday pay. They're on low incomes and zero-hour contracts. And that happens everywhere – even the NHS are doing that.'

'It's especially bad in the Christmas, Easter, summer holidays. Because a lot of those families, low-income ones, have been getting free school dinners so in the evening they'll have beans on toast, eggs on toast, because they've had a proper meal in the day. What're you going to do in the holidays then?'

I made a strange, sad noise. Of course, none of this was news to me but it hurt to see the reality of that theoretical hunger on those shelves lined with 'basics' – cans of beans, big packets of pasta and sweaty bags of white bread. I have the same reaction to pawn shops – I know they exist but I still tear up when I see one because of everything they represent to me. Because some things can shuttle me back in time like no years have passed at all.

One of the older men gestured to a woman standing at the back and told me that she always made sure the animals were fed too. She looked both shy and proud. 'Aye, well, I've got a dog myself and when I was down on my luck I'd still feed my dog. A pet's just part of your family.'

I told them how exceptional I thought their work was. How moving it was to know that in every community there were people like them doing work like this. Even though it shouldn't be needed at all.

'We're very lucky. There's even kids coming in with their piggy banks and opening them up for us.'

'We had a gentleman at Christmas time who said, "I've sat in the car for twenty minutes just trying to get the courage to come in." He was a well-dressed man, he worked, his marriage had just broken down and he'd had to pay for a few months' rent up front on his new place. And he was just mortified, it was breaking his heart. So, I sat with him and we gave him his food and gave him extra in case he didn't want to come back. I told him, "Don't be afraid to come back, and save your money for your electric meter and for your gas."'

They asked me when the book would be out and I told them not until next year.

'I've got to write it yet!'

'I might no' be around by then,' one joker said.

We laughed and they told me more stories.

'This woman, she worked for M&S and her husband stole her wages and took the kids' computers to sell. And that was the second time he'd done that. So she came in here to get the babies food. And she did work, she worked hard. She got him arrested and chucked him out in the end.'

'There's a man who had his own profitable business and it went bust and suddenly he had nothing.'

'And another who was a season worker, roofing, and he couldn't get any work and he'd still to feed his family.'

'There were two girls, one in college and the other in school, and their mum just left. They didn't have anything, no sanitary towels, nothing, and they'd never told anyone. They'd just kept going because they were too proud. I remember the social worker was distraught telling me.'

I thought about how bad something must be to shock a social worker in this day and age. I wanted to tell them I understood, only too well. 'I think a lot of the people who have a prejudice about poverty are people who don't realise just how close we all are to it.'

'Aye, just a few wages away. It could happen to us all.'

I asked them what might turn around a place like Coatbridge. What might make it better for those who were struggling.

'Honestly, there's nothing in Coatbridge to change. It comes from above, the government. Like we were saying earlier, it's the sanctions. We had a woman who had cancer and she had her treatment at the hospital the same day as her benefits appointment and she was sanctioned for going to her treatment. It's not here in Coatbridge that's the problem.'

They invited me to stay for some sandwiches, and while it would have made me happy to spend more time in their kind, gently heckling company, I said I wanted to have a walk around the town while the snow held off.

There was a woman in reception as I was leaving. She was perhaps in her fifties, though it was difficult to tell her age since she had that hard, prematurely weary face I've seen on many women from my background. She was slightly hunched, turned towards a volunteer who filled out a clipboard enthusiastically and efficiently, trying to make her feel comfortable, knowing what it must have cost her to simply step through the doors.

'Just anything, anything at all that you've got . . .'

'And have you any pets at home?'

'Aye, I've two dogs.'

'Well, we'll get them something too.'

I waved goodbye quickly, scared I might cry in the face of that woman's hurt and difficulty, which wasn't even mine to be crying for in the first place.

Up the road, outside a garage, lying in a hollowed footstep in the snow, I found a ten-pound note. I picked it up and turned it over. I held it, I couldn't possibly take it. I retraced my steps to give it in to the foodbank and then couldn't quite face going back and seeing that woman. I thought about waiting and giving it to her but didn't want her to feel the hot/cold, grateful/shameful burn of charity I remember so well. In the end I simply put it back where it lay, knowing she'd have to walk this way when she left, desperately hoping she'd see it.

Ten quid. An amount I sometimes spend on coffee and a slice of cake without even blinking. How comparatively little that seems to me now. I'd forgotten how much money that could feel like. How having a single note in your purse could feel like a buoy in a wild, stormy sea. Once I remembered it, I felt it in the pit of my belly, in the ache of my cold bones. I started walking towards Coatbridge's town centre where half the shops were boarded up.

*

I was late. I needed coffee. I needed something to wash down the two tiny pink beta blockers, like pencil erasers, that I take when I know I'm frightened. I walked up through the high-rises of Motherwell. I knew the way but I was surprised by how drab the building looked. It must have been new twenty-five years ago. I remembered it on sunnier days. But the squat, grubby yellow-brick New Light Church now looked like an old folks' home that had seen better days.

The service had already started when I walked in. A plump smiling woman in an eighties jumper greeted me.

'I'm sorry I'm a wee bit late,' I said. I gestured towards the noises in the next room. 'Can I . . . I wondered if I could . . . attend the service?'

The woman looked startled then delighted, and ushered me in. I don't imagine walk-ins are something they experience much of.

It was surprising how comforting it felt to enter that space after so many years. To walk through the tables laid out for coffee and squash afterwards and down to the congregation area, which was sparsely occupied.

Some older folk turned and smiled and I smiled in return, the warmth both a physical and emotional relief. But as I walked towards the congregation I noticed a little boy onstage, maybe four years old, holding a microphone while beaming adults hovered above him and the band gently strummed an electric guitar and played brushes on the cymbals. I didn't catch what the boy said except that it was about being saved. That he was talking about God. Occasionally someone shouted out 'Yes, Lord' and then the pastor took away the mic and said the equivalent of 'Out of the mouth of babes. God is good.' And everyone applauded.

It was very affecting. It was absolute horseshit. That tiny kid learning about sin and a devil and how he could please God before he learned to tie his shoelaces. Any comfort I felt in being there or any guilt or doubt as to whether I'd introduce myself afterwards disappeared. My coffee seemed to be turning bitter in my stomach.

I sat at the edge of a pew on the far side of the room. The church was far emptier than it had ever been in my day. Perhaps the snow. But perhaps not. 'I wonder if anyone will recognise you,' Sally had said the previous day (she hadn't wanted to come with me), and I said I didn't think they would but then became nervous sitting there. Someone passed along a printout with a few questions and a space to take notes about the sermon and I gladly occupied myself writing things down.

We sang rock ballads (one I'd be humming for months afterwards) and I lowered my head and closed my eyes for prayer which reminded me a little of the mindfulness meditation I'd come to love. The sermon was on the theme of 'Take Courage' from the Book of Joshua but I didn't take much in. I felt deeply uncomfortable, though the warm room and gentle guitar should have been soothing, and eventually gathered my own courage and left early with the congregation staring after me as I went.

The sleet was horizontal and I wrapped my scarf around my head and walked towards the car park where Sally was waiting for me.

'That was so weird. So weird. I had my first kiss on those steps right there. I can't believe we used to come here.'

'I know. It's mental.'

And we both shook our heads in a 'what the fuck was that?' manner and then drove to the pub. Once there we both ordered, without comment, macaroni cheese and then realised we'd entirely regressed. We talked about our pasts but mainly our presents: her teenage daughter, my approaching wedding, the places we'd been, our love lives.

We were still a little bashful with each other but we ate and drank while she told me more about raising her daughter by herself, how well the girl had just done in her exams.

'How about you?' she asked. 'Have you ever thought about it?'

I took a long drink of my beer, thought of my mum, my grandmothers, my sister, of that little boy onstage today. The thing that had shifted in Aberdeen while standing in my old school playground watching that mother and baby hadn't moved back to wherever it had come from. I'd always been terrified about the idea of being a mother, too afraid of hurting the child inside myself to even think of it. But, somehow, things were changing.

'Actually, I really don't know how I feel about it.'

Afterwards she drove me to her flat and introduced me to her daughter – a beautiful fifteen-year-old who was doing her maths homework and who, alarmingly, seemed more grown up than we were. I cuddled her hairless kitten called Rudi who felt a little like a very affectionate old man who had been shrunk along with his pink polo neck. We drank tea, then Sally drove me to the station where she waved me off as I went back down those concrete steps. Just like we were fifteen again.

21
Great Yarmouth
1995

'Why do you hate him so much?'

'Because whenever he's about things get worse.'

I knew this was true about Richie but when he arrived back in Coatbridge from Great Yarmouth even I was pleased to see him. He arrived in a bright orange eighties car that he'd 'borrowed' from a pal. Me and Mum pissed ourselves laughing as he got out and lounged against the car, full of himself, like a North Lanark Knight Rider. I called it the Tangomobile.

It was the usual rush – a day, maybe two – to leave. It didn't take long to pack up. What we had could mostly be fitted into black bin bags and crisp boxes scavenged from the local shop, or it was so shite it wasn't worth driving it the length of the country. My sister was thrilled to see her da. Mum was thrilled too, maybe just at the prospect of another of those new starts or simply because the neighbours would see we weren't all alone after all.

Me? I'd known I was on a hiding to nothing in Coatbridge and, besides, it wasn't a hard place to give up. In Great Yarmouth, I'd decided, I'd be different, I'd be cool. I'd make friends and keep them. I thought I'd get into surfing and have a tan like the girls on *Home and Away*.

It was a rough journey down to Great Yarmouth, all four of us squeezed into the Tangomobile, surrounded by our boxes and bags and the sweaty odours of August. We broke down halfway, Mum and Richie rowed, and we slept in a lay-by, legs twisted and tangled until we could get towed in the morning to a garage. Where we admitted we'd no money to pay and Mum had no choice but to leave our dog-eared, soft cream benefits books as insurance that we'd settle the bill. I remember vividly us all squatting down by the side of the car, streams of piss interweaving, and then cruising through the grey suburbs of Great Yarmouth with all of that initial optimism as empty as our bladders.

I don't remember what we ate that night, but I know we had no money until the next day when the benefits office opened, and we could get an emergency loan and Mum could request replacement books. We were kipping with Richie until Mum could register as homeless. He'd not mentioned, or perhaps he had and Mum had ignored the fact, that his place was a studio barely big enough to unfold its dubiously stained sofa bed. Perhaps the thinking was that the worse our accommodation was the sooner we'd be rehomed.

His studio was in one of the large grubby cream villas on the seafront that had been converted over to hostels for the waifs and strays who arrived for work each summer season and then stayed on for winter when the work was gone, since where else would they go?

Through the windows we could hear the repetitive sing-song of the Sea Life Centre's tannoy, and the occasional holidaymaker's overexcited scream. The first thing Richie told us not to do was put our hands down the back of the sofa.

'What would we do that for anyway?'

'Never mind. Just don't. There's dirty needles down there.'

The second thing he told us was we weren't to speak to any of the other people in the building.

So there we were. Fourteen-year-old me, my seven-year-old sister, my mum and her ex-husband in a space no bigger than my bedroom in Coatbridge with the Sea Life Centre blasting its opening times, me and Richie arguing the toss on everything, and Mum, as usual, looking around and wondering what the fuck we'd got ourselves into. It was an uncomfortable few days.

That first week Mum got us a space in a B&B that accepted housing benefit. Two streets back from the seafront, it was one of a row of terraced houses with hanging baskets and 'Rooms to Let' signs. For all of our housing benefit, plus a bit more from our child benefit, we got two small adjoining rooms, one with a double bed and another with a single, a shared bathroom and kitchen, and a black-and-white TV. I only remember meeting one other tenant, a man in his fifties who told us we shouldn't leave our toilet paper in the shared bathroom or it would be stolen.

It was August 1995 and Great Yarmouth was not quite the ghost town it would become over the next few years. I killed a lot of time wandering around by myself. I wove in and out of the tourists and went and flicked through CDs in the local record shop, Prism Records. I went to a shop called Slippery Dicks and stared up longingly at the band T-shirts. I wanted to be an artist or a writer and spent a lot of time drawing with biro in my notebook and starting a novel about a sassy female mechanic called Kat who all the boys fancied.

It was Mum who said I was old enough to get a job and that she wanted me out of the B&B. So, I went from restaurant to restaurant asking for work until the last place I tried, a big, dirt-cheap cafe specialising in set dinners and kiddies' meals took me on as a waitress for £1.50 an hour. I was a terrible waitress. I once spilled an entire bowl of spotted dick and custard on an old man's lap. I wasn't 'pretty' by most men's standards, with my glasses and no boobs, but the ponytailed manager thought I had a nice arse ('Even you can appreciate that,' he'd say to our gay chef as I bent for bread rolls) and I worked all the hours they wanted for cheap.

I made friends with a waitress in her twenties who'd moved down from Scotland and was living in a B&B, and together we'd drink halves of lager and lime with the chefs after our shifts, and smoke grass back in her room which was entirely empty except for our scattered shoes and her make-up bag. I bought a bag of grass from one of the chefs and when Mum found it she laughed her head off because they'd sold me a bag of oregano. Mum knew I was drinking and smoking dope and out all hours. I don't know if she was too overwhelmed by me to cope but I suspect it was more that she couldn't bear to be at war with me. She wanted to be my pal, not my mother.

I will never forget getting that first little brown envelope of soft twenties from that job. That rich feeling. I treated Mum to cream cakes and tea at one of the nicer cafes and took my sister for ice cream and to the Sea Life Centre. I bought myself some clothes for school from New Look and oil pastels and a sketchpad. It wasn't much but it was more than I'd ever had. The freedom of that money, of knowing that while I had a salary I could go places, have things I needed – wanted even – that I'd never be hungry while I earned, that was what that first shitty job taught me.

It also taught me about putting up with whatever was meted out. About not making a fuss, unless you were already leaving, and to make sure they didn't screw you on your last pay packet. About how vulnerable those jobs made you and how low others viewed you as. About checks and balances, of control and submission. In a perverse way, I was lucky I could subjugate myself so easily and put up with being shouted at, having things thrown at me, with leering comments and wandering hands, being spat on and called bitch and whore over a few quid's worth of tips. Most people couldn't, and I don't blame them at all. If you wonder why those on the margins sometimes seem averse to work, to taking whatever work they can (even though this is very rarely the case), it's because the shittier the pay, the harder the work, the shittier you are treated. In those jobs you are treated as people see you, as grudgingly necessary but expendable and far, far beneath everyone else.

For twenty-four years I grafted hard in jobs I was lucky to get because I knew how to charm and lie my way to people giving me a go, because I had a knack for learning quick, I kept my mouth shut, and found that the longer hours I did, the more I got used to that bone-weary feeling. Because, as my mum would say, 'my face fitted'. I was blonde and smiley, I knew what they wanted and I gave it.

From the age of fourteen to my fast-approaching thirty-eighth birthday I have never not worked. Even at my very sickest, when I was so ill with anxiety I cried in every private moment and my whole body coated itself with psoriasis as though armouring itself against attack, I worked and worked. Call centres, a Harrods Christmas elf, plenty more waitressing, chambermaiding, shop work, cleaning toilets, street fundraising, nannying, care work, eventually work with charities, from answering the phones to being responsible for raising over a million quid. And all the while I listened to people, who'd never lived a day of the sort of life I'd had, say my sort were work-shy and scroungers.

Given the opportunity I don't think I would take those jobs and take that much shit again.

I probably would have stayed working if I could have, but the holiday season was almost finished. Suddenly, Great Yarmouth emptied out and the grab arcade machines playing 'Oh my Darling Clementine' echoed off the empty pavements, pubs were empty, the crowd outside the jobcentre was much bigger.

Mum chose my school because she'd met two nice-seeming

teen lads and had asked them where they went. So, I ended up taking a bus each day from Great Yarmouth to Caister High School. Nowhere in that area is well off but Caister Village was, in comparison to Great Yarmouth, a more middle-class area. Neat houses with carefully tended gardens and family cars in the driveways. My schoolmates lived in houses their families owned, their parents ferried them about and they never wanted for money to spend on clothes at the weekend. It would have been a good choice of school, except that, of course, the fact I was poor and different stood out more than ever.

At first, I did OK. Turns out Scotland wasn't only a year ahead in the school curriculum but also in wayward teen behaviour, and the fact I'd smoked dope, that my mum would buy us cider to drink on a Friday night before the roller disco at the Winter Gardens, and that I wasn't a virgin, stood me in good stead. I made friends with a group of middling-popular girls. And, to their credit, not only did they accept me, they even visited our dingy two rooms to drink those two-litre bottles of cider and didn't spread it all around school that I lived in a shit B&B and shared a room with my mum. Which was pretty miraculous.

But they were too well behaved for me and, with my love of Alanis Morissette and Green Day and drinking as much as I could, I was too weird and wired for them. I got into drama and started going out drinking with the amateur dramatics group I joined (a special note of acknowledgment here goes to the men in their thirties and forties who bought my drinks). I started going to Great Yarmouth's many nightclubs. I was learning quickly that the greatest measure of my value was how fanciable I was. I knew a short skirt, the promise of sex in the showing of skin, would up my value a little at least. At Peggotty's Bar, where me and my new pals from school went most often, they did a black bottle of K cider for 99p and if you went and danced on the pool table the DJ gave you a bottle of 'champagne' to drink as you snaked your hips.

By this time, me, Mum and my sister had moved into a tiny lean-to house on a square next to a car park. It had three 'flats', if by flat you mean a minuscule living room with a cooker and a mouldy fridge wedged in, a 'bedroom' entirely taken up with a double and single bed, and a shower room where literal mushrooms grew from the skirting boards.

We had rented it from a private landlord which meant a top-up payment, but we were so glad to have separate rooms to sleep and live in we were overjoyed. Our neighbours were a man in his fifties who I thought was taking a fatherly interest in me when he brought me presents until Mum told me, hooting away, he had a crush on me. And a Welsh guy downstairs who had a problem with glue sniffing. We'd hear him bellowing angrily to himself, furniture crashing, while we tried to concentrate on *EastEnders*.

The two girls from school I'd started hanging out with went out with some boys at the homeless hostel near my house. Since I was poor and weird and not particularly pretty they allowed me to tag along because I was no competition or threat, given their early blossoming, acid tongues and traffic-stopping beauty. Plus, they could always say they were staying at my house and I could always get booze.

We went out to clubs in a big gang. I was never really part of the group, but I liked even being on the edges of it. I kissed and slept with a few of the guys, in rooms with a microwave, a bare mattress, dirty ashtrays and nothing else. They never had more than the cost of a drink on a Saturday and, in their late teens, they were probably deeply troubled themselves. But to us they were big, older men paying us attention, and to them we were admirers who made them feel big and older and who they occasionally got to fuck too.

I would have probably done OK, despite the drinking and fucking and the shitty house and no money and Mum's problems. Except, then I fell out with those girls. Then the rumours started. Teenage girls are the most vengeful I've ever known. If I wanted to hire assassins I'd choose only teenage girls with an axe to grind. Once the rumours started at school, once everyone witnessed me retreating down the social pecking order to hang with the poor, chubby, odd kids, then it was open season.

I have never particularly defined myself by the fact that I was bullied for much of my school life but I'm sure it burrowed in somewhere deep and comes out in the way I hold my life and mind together as an adult. Perhaps the issue was that once it had started it escalated so quickly because I never found a way not to be hurt, not to be furious, not to wear all my emotions on the surface of my skin.

So, I was called everything under the sun. I was a slag, a slut, I was smelly, I had Aids, I was a lezzer. People walked on my heels all the way to class, they all deliberately swapped seats to avoid me, they stabbed pencils and compasses into my back during maths classes and then grinned at me when I turned round tearfully begging them to stop. My clothes, my body, my face, the way I spoke. If I was too smart or seemed stupid. Almost every moment of every day in school there was someone letting me know that they hated me, that they found everything about me disgusting, that everyone else did too. Seven hours a day, five days a week, lasting for years.

I went to a teacher and told him, sobbing, that I was being bullied, and I didn't care what would happen, I needed to be moved from that maths class. He said I could only be moved to the remedial class and so that's where I was sent. Perhaps he meant well, but that same teacher stood by as another male teacher looked at my skirt and said to him, 'I smell fish,' while waving his hand through the air. I presume he was thinking of my pubic hair.

I called my dad one night, weeping, Mum hovering just by my shoulder. Please, I begged him, please can I come and stay with you and start a new school in London? I told him, they bully me, everyone hates me, I can't stand it. He said no. Why not? I asked, and he told me he wasn't able to care for me. Mum looked satisfied and I cried so much my face was all swollen the next day.

Finally, mercifully, the summer holidays came. I remember crying with relief on the bus home. We'd moved by this time into another place, a two-up two-down, with an en suite bathroom and a second toilet in the kitchen, in a residential area just outside town. It was freezing and damp in places, it was sparse and it was far, far better than anything we'd had in a long time. I went to the library, set in a concrete building next to the DSS and the family-planning clinic, and got stacks of books that I'd carry tilted up my body the full twenty-minute walk home. I read everything I could lay my hands on, whether I had a horrific hangover or if Mum was raging or if I was heartbroken because no one had called me to go out.

In nightclubs I'd shout over the 'Return of the Mack' and ask men twice my age who were fondling my arse cheeks through the cheap polyester of my dress whether they had read Truman Capote, while trying not to spill my pint of snakebite. You can imagine how that went down. I kept a tally of how many men I got off with each night, which was usually more than ten but less than twenty. I slept with one of the most popular boys in our school, a boy who'd never spoken to me or acknowledged me, under a pier. He pulled out my tampon, threw it by my head, pumped away for a few minutes and then left me lying in the sand next to my bloody tampon and the used condom while he went back to the club. He never spoke to me or acknowledged me after.

I got a summer job in a Greek-Cypriot family's cafe and spent my time there singing to the radio and serving mugs of tea the colour of the American tan tights my grandma used to wear. I spent my pay cheques on more little dresses, on make-up, on Sun In that turned my hair a crispy yellow I thought was gorgeous. I got myself contact lenses and spent a lot of money in tanning booths. I didn't really have a set of friends that summer so only occasionally went out with whoever would have me. But I was working and had money and men beeped at me from passing cars. I was reading library books that gave me the idea that I might have a better sort of life if I could escape the suck of the town. I visited my dad in his new halfway house for recovering alcoholics in Westbourne Grove, heard every different language on the streets around there and told him I wanted to live in London when I was old enough.

I was the very riskiest of combinations: hopeful, hurting, vulnerable, newly aware of my sexual power and very, very lonely.

I don't know that I have ever felt a feeling of dread as strong, of a situation that felt as inescapable, as going back to school that year. My saving graces were the group of goths and geeks that I started to hang around with and drama, English and art classes. Walking into those classrooms meant I wouldn't be bullied for an hour, I could do something I liked and, crucially, something that gave me hope I might go off and do something else. That I might leave Great Yarmouth and all those people behind and reinvent myself.

I lived for Friday nights at the Brunswick. The 'Brunny' had three floors. The top floor, where I used to go in my tiny mini-dresses and once split my knee open on smashed glass and kept dancing all night regardless, played pop music. The middle floor

was for live bands and for middle-aged men nursing pints and grop-
ing your arse as you went by. The basement was called 'The Crypt'
and was painted entirely black with walls that dripped with sweat
and cheap beer. It played indie, retro, metal and grunge. It was full
of weirdos and misfits. It was, for someone looking for their tribe, a
revelation. We still went out to other places, Ocean Rooms on
Thursdays, the Garibaldi or Bourbon Street on Saturdays, but The
Crypt was where it felt like life might really be happening and it
might be a life I actually wanted.

It was there that I met Lisa, a twenty-eight-year-old single
mum to an eight-year-old boy. It started when I went back to her
flat, which was just around the corner from the Brunswick, with
some others. There were twelve years between us, but we became
inseparable. She was a hippie and an ex-biker. She had a temper,
she could match me drink for drink and was always up for a party.
I think she was a bit stuck for mates who wanted to go out, she
liked younger guys nearer my age and so we glued ourselves to
each other.

I celebrated my sixteenth birthday with her but can't remember much else about it. We slept with the guys from the bands who
played at the Brunswick. We were perfect wing-women. I basically
lived at her flat and things with Mum deteriorated further and further. Mum once called the police to go searching for me though I'd
often spent whole days and nights away before. And one day when
I *did* come home, there was a coat covering a patch of pink vomit
where she'd drunk a whole bottle of cherry brandy.

Lisa was great fun, she was the first friend I'd ever really loved,
she was often maternal, she was flirtatious. We slept in the same
bed, had sex in it at the same time and kissed each other more
than once. She could be possessive too, jealous, both of me paying
attention to guys, and guys paying attention to me. It was all as

heady, exhilarating and tumultuous as first love, especially for a schoolgirl who had spent her whole life desperately lonely. Except, of course, she was twelve years older than me and it also wasn't quite right.

She started going out with a beautiful but troubled sixteen-year-old boy called Simon. For a while they seemed happy, and our friendship evened out to parties and dancing and hung-over mugs of tea while we discussed the sex we'd had the previous night and she regaled me with stories of her youth.

So, I had a secret life. During the week I pulled on my school uniform and did my best to get through each day as unscathed as possible. I stayed quiet, I walked the corridors at lunchtime so I wasn't a sitting duck, I stopped absorbing anything in class unless it was in English or drama, where I knew the teachers would stick up for me and where, for some reason, the kids never taunted me anyway.

In my evenings I went to Lisa's house and we drank tea and wine, watched *Friends* and gossiped. We went out on weekends and walked around bars and clubs like we owned them, the first up dancing. I loved to get men to want me but whenever one was decent, and really interested in going out with me, I dropped them cold.

In one part of my life I was careening, too bright and too young, too much in need of something to mend the cracks. And in another I was constantly pummelled. One fed the other. I drank more and more at the weekends, fucked more men, and during the week retreated further and further from school, friends my own age, and everything else that might be considered normal. If Mum noticed, her greatest resentment was that Lisa now held more sway than her. If school noticed, I didn't see any sign of it. There was no one else to care.

I suppose I was learning in my own way. I learned that a man in his twenties would enjoy you repeating that you were only fifteen while you gave him a clumsy handjob. I learned that too drunk was never too drunk for men and that age was no barrier (I never lied about it and it never stopped anyone). I learned that fights were inevitable. Once the mother and sister of a guy I'd only kissed took against me and one held me down while the other kicked me with her white plastic platforms. I had to go to A&E the next day and get an injection like an epidural. Mum was disgusted with me (she never quite saw the link between her own drinking and mine) and refused to accept I couldn't get out of bed. She pulled me out forcibly, despite my screaming as my back spasmed, and, because I had no option and no money, I hobbled to Lisa's where I slept on her sofa for two weeks, off my head on co-proxamol, until Mum apologised and I went home.

I learned how expendable a commodity sex was and how powerful. I learned that girls our age could get pregnant fast when every girl in my small, transient circle ended up pregnant within a year. I learned to project myself in a certain way – tough, mouthy. I learned that a shitstorm was always round the corner, so I might as well sink myself in a sea of booze and let it take me where it would in the meantime.

I don't think it was one particular thing that made me decide. It was only two, maybe three months before I was due to take my GCSEs and in spite of everything my grades were all predicted As and Bs (except for maths obviously). I wanted to go to university in London. I had auditioned for and got a place on a drama course at the nearest college already.

I just woke up one weekend morning and knew I couldn't go back to that daily torture. I told Mum while we were eating spaghetti bolognese on the Sunday night in front of the TV. I told her I had a plan, I'd go to college somewhere and get qualifications but if I had to go back to school for another two months I'd likely kill myself.

I don't know whether I ever really felt I would have but I know that dealing with that daily degradation was something I couldn't cope with any more. Of all the hard, painful things that have ever happened in my life I consider being trapped in a space with peers who turn against you to be the very worst. Even writing this I shake.

So, I stopped. I got a job as a waitress since the summer season was just starting. I used my wages to go out and drink more. Amazingly, only one teacher – the English teacher Mr Collar – called to see where I was. By then I'd already found out I could spend the next year studying a few GCSEs at Norwich City College. So I thanked him for calling but didn't tell him how instrumental his kindness, genuine enthusiasm and interest had been for me. Mr Collar, if you read this, thank you so much.

22
Great Yarmouth
1997

That summer brought the first of the sexual assaults. Two friends and I were walking home from a night out together. We were less drunk than usual – these girls, who I met while working, were the same age as me and didn't drink as much as Lisa and I did. It was gone 2 a.m. but as long as we walked in a group and through residential streets we'd never seen the harm.

The first thing that happened was that a white transit van drove past us. Not so strange in itself except that it was the wee hours and we were in a narrow side street near my house where traffic barely went even in the daytime. We thought nothing of it, we were in high spirits, talking about the night, about our plans for the week.

When he jumped out of the alley, only fifty yards from my front door, he was wearing a stocking on his face. For half a second, I thought I might laugh, perhaps I did, because surely rapists only wore stockings on their faces in films.

Everything stopped. It was my mum's voice I heard. All her stories of the bogeymen finally coming true. I heard her as clearly as if she was there shouting, 'Scream and run. You hear me? Anyone tries to grab you, you scream and run.' So, I started screaming for help and ran towards my door. When I turned, I saw one of my friends being pushed to the ground, the man on top of her and the other girl pulling and kicking at him. A neighbour opened their window and started shouting at us, I ran back, still screaming for help. The man took fright and ran. We limped back to my mum's house, hysterical and shaking.

It was in the local newspaper, the *Advertiser*, a few column inches. He'd torn right through my friend's shorts. Everyone said we'd been lucky, but I was too scared to leave the house for a week and shook uncontrollably when I did. I had to walk past that alley almost every day to go anywhere I wanted to. Eventually I bounced back, or thought I did, as did my friends. But we weren't friends any more. I think they thought I'd been trying to run away. And perhaps I had. Scream and then run – I'd been taught well.

I started Norwich City College to study for my English, drama and art GCSEs that September. It was probably the happiest I'd ever been. I sensed a sort of opening up of the future. I wore paratrooper boots and carried around a cherry-red army bag. I ostentatiously read *Melody Maker* and sat cross-legged on chairs.

Each day I woke at 6.30 a.m. and took the bus through tiny villages to a proper city. An anonymous city, where I'd walk to a big college full of students who didn't know me and where those that did liked me. I made friends quickly, I knew the right bands, had the right clothes, I had older friends and went out all the time. Those students, mostly from nice homes in provincial suburbs and villages, thought of me as a party girl. I suppose I was.

But I also loved learning. I loved walking around with my folders held to my chest and reading my plays and books sitting in corridors around the campus. Finally, I was in classes where people had chosen to be there. My drama and English teachers encouraged me. My English teacher told me I was a natural writer and I was thrilled, my fingers prickling in pleasure, but laughed her off. I was terrible at art and gave it up – just as I always have whenever I've encountered something I'm not good at.

I spent more time in Norwich with my college friends – which both Mum and Lisa disliked with varying degrees of subtlety.

On my seventeenth birthday my dad sent me a full-length beaded evening dress. Lisa wrapped up seventeen little presents, including a furry red Elmo rucksack. I danced all night in The Crypt and it seemed everything was going to be OK.

But, like I said, you never knew when the next shitstorm would hit and mine were all coming at once.

There were two more assaults. The first happened outside Lisa's block of flats at 7.30 at night. I pressed the buzzer, felt someone behind me and then a hand clamped between my legs. I opened my mouth to scream but nothing came out and when I whipped my head around I looked into the eyes of a man wearing a black ski mask and a jumper that looked like it had been bought at Glastonbury ('the type of jumper hippies wear' is what I think I called it in my police statement). Scream. Run. So, I screamed. 'Get the fuck off me.' But it wasn't so much a scream as a breathless whisper. Nonetheless, whatever fury he saw in my eyes meant he ran, not me.

I called the police because I had been taught that's what you should do to stop them from doing it to others. They came and dutifully, if dubiously, took my statement, referring to my 'bad luck' lately. They must have thought I was 'one of those girls', but I took them at their word and said I thought I'd actually been very lucky. I'd escaped twice.

A few months later the man turned himself in to the police because there was a spate of violent sexual assaults happening in the next town and he was scared it would be pinned on him. They found his hippie jumper. He was found guilty of my assault and a few others – though he'd never raped anyone. The female police officer who came to tell me about his confession and double-check my statement apologised for her colleagues, but I didn't understand until a decade later what she meant.

Next, walking home from college, I heard a voice behind me and when I turned I saw a fat middle-aged bloke who had his limp dick in his hand and was taking steps towards me and shouting at me (bitch, I think). I screamed back (it came naturally by now) and ran but it wasn't in fear. I wondered if my whole life would be this way, if that's what being a woman was. When I told my mum she said, 'It's the way you walk about. I can see what they see with your blonde ponytail bobbing.' She said, 'I'm worried you'll never get over this.' But she and everyone else underestimated my desire to live, leave, escape. I didn't tell the police that time though.

I still drank prodigiously. If anything, college had increased my drinking since suddenly it was fine to go and drink in the afternoons at the tiny student union and then go on to bars. If I had money I was drinking.

I got my GCSEs, an A in drama and two A*s in English language and literature and enrolled for A levels and a GCSE in maths at the college the next year. I still had my plan to go to university in London.

Great Yarmouth was temporary, a place with no opportunities I'd be leaving soon enough, and so, I figured, I might as well scorch the earth while I was still there.

I slept again with the man – let's call him Steve – who had once asked me to repeat over and over that I was fifteen as I gave him a handjob. There were a few reasons for this. One was that I was now two years older and keen to impress him after he'd dismissed me as a fifteen-year-old (good enough for a handjob but not much else), and another was that I was a seventeen-year-old girl with a vacuum where my self-esteem should have been, he was popular in our crowd, and him wanting me made me feel special. At the time I had just started dating a twenty-eight-year-old man who lived and worked in London. He owned his own home, worked as a consultant. He was decent to me – if we avoid the dubiousness of a man of nearly thirty pursuing a teen – he had said he'd wait until I was ready for sex. I slept with Steve again because I was worried I wouldn't be good enough at sex for a proper grown-up with a proper job who treated me nicely and took trains from London to see me.

The day after, with Steve's sperm still swimming around in me, I went and met my new consultant boyfriend and his father (who, I remember, sweetly wore sandals and socks) with a hangover crafted by the devil himself, and soon I'd be pregnant.

I make no excuses for getting pregnant. I was drunk and stupid. I was very drunk. So drunk that I almost fell over Steve's banisters while climbing up the stairs. But I remember clearly the moment when I decided to sleep with him again. Spinning around the dance floor of The Crypt in a paisley dress to the Police, feeling like my life was beginning, and seeing him watching me and feeling my skin run golden with the power of his wanting.

It was Lisa who asked me when I'd last had my period. We were in her kitchen joking about something over a cup of tea. I counted the dates. Even in adulthood I have never been good at keeping up with period dates, but it was obvious, as I counted the squares off on her cartoon-cow-themed wall calendar, I was at the very least a week late.

I did the test the next day alone in her flat while she was at work. I chose the cheapest test, I think I might even have borrowed the money for it. It was a strange old-fashioned device with a paper cup to pee in and a felt circle like a Polo mint to float in the piss. It might have been left over from the eighties, but it worked just fine. I was seventeen and pregnant.

I cried the whole night. Then I got up the next morning, went to the family planning clinic and booked a termination.

I had to wait until I was at least eight weeks for that termination. It knocked me into a black place. I felt sick and tired. I wanted to drink but didn't want to go out. It seemed that for all my big dreams and new confidence I was as stupid as everyone else. I didn't, even for a moment, doubt my decision – though every adult asked if I did at every appointment – but I was heartbroken at having to make it. I convinced myself it was a mass of cells, but I cried and cried and cried. Perhaps I'd just been given something I could finally weep for. Lisa got angry that I didn't want to go out to clubs any more and, as though she herself had put the embryo in my cervix, I cut off contact cold. I never spoke to her again.

I told my mum and said straight away that I was having a termination.

'I want to go to university. I want to go to London.'

What I didn't say was, I want to leave Great Yarmouth. I don't want to end up like you.

She told me, not unkindly, that hopefully I'd miscarry. She told me (and was right) that the sadistic fuckers on abortion wards would put people choosing to get rid of their pregnancies in beds next to women who've just lost their much wanted babies. I called about a private termination advertised in the back of a *Cosmopolitan* but once I heard the price I hung up embarrassed. Instead, Mum brought me glasses of cold gin while I sat and cried in a bath so hot my whole body turned blancmange pink. But nothing shifted.

When I had appointments, I told them the father was no one. That I'd been drunk. I wasn't ashamed of having the abortion. Rather, I thought it showed I was ambitious. That I didn't want to throw my life away when I could do so much with it. I turned my head rather than look at the scans.

On the day itself I had an Irish nurse with pulled-back frizzy red hair. I would be put out cold and it would be removed and it would all be over. Like getting a tooth extracted. I didn't realise I'd have to talk to people. That there'd be questions like hers. She asked me time and time again, her eyes bright, if I was certain I wanted to do this – did she use the term 'kill this baby'? I can't remember but she might as well have. Next to me was an older woman crying.

The anaesthetist was older and kind with me and even as he held my hand and counted backwards I wondered if he found me beautiful and whether he might fall in love with me. Poor, daft wee girl.

I woke to someone singing a Beautiful South song and then they wheeled me back to the ward. I was covered in saline solution and dried blood. I was tender, but I was OK. When I went home Mum put a blanket over me and made me rice pudding. It was over, or so I thought.

In the summer break I went down to London to attend a Camp America recruitment day after seeing a poster at college. It was at a huge conference centre in west London where American summer camps came to find counsellors to work for the summer. If you were lucky enough to be offered a position it came with return flights, visas, medical insurance and some pocket money at the end to go travelling with.

Most had come with their parents but I'd travelled down that morning by coach, trying not to get too dishevelled in my carefully chosen outfit of a pale blue blouse hugging my still gently round belly, my hair held up with chopsticks, Mary Janes that pinched my feet.

I don't think I read or slept or listened to music on the journey down. Only stared out of the window and imagined myself in

America. America – where everything happened, and so far away from Great Yarmouth.

In the vast halls there was row after row of tables with confident, earnest Americans in sweatshirts showing brochures or videos of the 'camp experience'. Many had boards pinned up with pictures of smiling kids and even happier teens.

I walked around talking to the camp directors and counsellors. We'd been told in our invitation letters to 'sell ourselves' and, God knows, I tried. But how could I imagine myself in a camp with two swimming pools? With a cinema and stables and sailing boats just for kids? Sitting on folding chairs in front of those people, my feet throbbing, made me feel they could see right through me. And perhaps they could. At one table a blonde with impossibly perfect teeth exclaimed with excitement, 'We're an equestrian camp!' And I replied politely, 'Oh, no thank you. I don't want to go to a religious summer camp.'

I walked away with their laughter battering at my back.

In the end I chatted with two softly spoken hippies who ran a 4-H camp – which stood for head, heart, hands and health – called Bear Hill, in New Hampshire. They told me half the kids were paying guests and half got free places and that I should be prepared, the camp itself was very basic.

'That's OK. That sounds perfect.'

I took the coach home full of hope and dreams of New York, diners, holiday romances and all the places I'd travel after my summer in the mountains. Was this it? I thought. Was this the beginning of it all?

But that promise of a happier future was almost a whole year away and I was still struggling to deal with the events of the previous months. I can't say with certainty what effect the termination had on me but in a year I'd been involved in three sexual assaults, undergone a termination and stopped speaking to the best friend I ever had. I only told one person on my A-level course about my abortion, a lovely bisexual boy called David, a foster-kid, who'd lived alone since he was sixteen. On my eighteenth birthday he took me for a burger and pint at Wetherspoon's. I cried, and he held my hands platonically across the sticky tabletop.

I started to drink even more but perhaps that goes without saying. A levels were much harder than I'd thought and I slipped further and further behind. I had some friends in Norwich but none in Great Yarmouth any more, so I spent most weekends at home with Mum and my sister in our little living room watching *Wheel of Fortune* and *Casualty*. As I struggled to keep up with classes I began to realise that my dream of university in London was just that.

One weekend a friend came from Norwich to go out in Great Yarmouth. I wore a rainbow of tiny butterfly clips in my hair, combat trousers and a belly top. I was low and wanted to be looked at again, to feel special. That night, for better or worse, changed my life.

A few years after, I would call it 'this thing that happened'. About a decade later I learned to call it a 'sort of rape'. Now, I have done enough reading – occasionally, I even go on the Internet and look up the legal definition to be sure – to be able to actually say, 'I was raped.'

Except that I don't. I find it painful, horrifying to even write the words. After all, I wasn't pulled into an alley by a man in a ski mask. I wasn't preyed upon by an older relative. It wasn't me fighting him off tooth and nail. And, perhaps if I'd been a bit less drunk, I would have readily consented. I'd done that enough times before. But I did not consent, and I wasn't just drunk – I was immobile and he was violent.

I don't remember most of it. I think he had a moustache but that's also the sort of detail the memory might make up about a sexual predator. For some reason, I don't know why, he'd taken me back to another man's house who we'd met earlier that night though he didn't know him. When my friend arrived at the house he had me naked on the carpet of the living room face down. As soon as they arrived he ran out the door and into the night.

The next morning when I woke, I found I had wet myself. My vagina was red raw, and I had bruises, fingerprints, all over my thighs and buttocks and arms. Too afraid my friend and the guy whose house it was would realise I'd wet myself as soon as I stood up, from the smell and the stain, I stayed for far longer than I should have at that house. We smoked a lot of dope. The guy said he didn't know him and checked to see I hadn't told him where I lived or given him my phone number and I deadpanned, 'I don't think he's the calling type.'

After we left my friend, who was sweet-natured but scatty, tried to talk to me about what had happened and I told her to shut up and stormed home. At home, waiting for me, was my acceptance to the Camp America programme. My dreamed-of travel and adventure and escape. It hurt to sit down on the sofa and I was so stoned I could barely open the envelope.

I reasoned for years and years to myself that since I so often slept with strangers when drunk, on beaches and down alleys and in strange rooms, it shouldn't matter about him.

But it mattered because I didn't choose. It mattered because my body understood it had been violated. It matters still.

A few weeks later I had to get off the bus to college and be sick in the street. I was pregnant again.

*

I didn't tell the police. I didn't know I should. If he had been wearing a mask. If I'd had proper injuries. If my friend and that guy had seen me struggling (though I don't know that they didn't) then I might have. But I doubt it. I didn't tell my mum, I thought she'd say it was my own fault. Which is how I felt. I'm ashamed to say, even after a lot of thinking and therapy and tearful 2 a.m. talks with people who love me, I still think that to a small extent, though I know that's bullshit.

This time there were no sympathetic words, no kindnesses for the pregnant teen. When the family planning clinic, doctors, my mum, asked me who the father was I said, truthfully, I was so drunk I couldn't remember. None of them asked further questions. They simply raised their eyebrows or gave me a stern lecture on contraception – I couldn't just keep having abortions rather than using condoms, they told me.

Had they asked me if I had been raped I don't think I would have said yes. I was in extreme denial myself. Though I knew, I absolutely knew, something unforgivable had been done to my body. As though my body knew this too, I was cursed with extreme morning sickness. I couldn't eat and threw up only stringy bile or alarming froth. Eventually, I went to the doctor for pills and she, again, told me off for my recklessness. I shouted at her that I wasn't stupid, it was an accident, I was going to university. My mum shouted at me in turn.

The more I cried, the more I was sick, the more vulnerable I became, the angrier Mum was, the more she demanded I didn't just lie around. She told me that the sound of me waking in the morning, and having to face me, made her sick to her stomach.

I don't remember the second abortion. I do remember they put a birth control implant into my arm. I was still woozy and, though they had explained, I had no idea what it was or what the side effects might be. There were no blankets or rice pudding afterwards. I begged to take a taxi, the huge NHS pad sticking to my thighs, but Mum told me we were catching the yellow-and-green 'banana bus' that went around the estates. She said, 'What I did wrong was give you treats. Well, you'll get no treats now.'

I got an infection and bled for weeks. I lay around in the stinking dressing gown I'd had for years and numbly watched TV. Mum lost her temper with me each day and I replied that soon I was going to America and she wouldn't have to see me at all. One way or another, I had lost all of my friends.

I knew I needed work if I was going to have spending money for America and so, though it was early in the season, I quit college, which I was failing badly anyway, and went from shop to shop looking for a job. I worked in a hot-dog kiosk attached to an amusement arcade. I got twenty pounds a day for frying up sausages while the arcade games droned on and on. I worked in a toy shop where my only job was to stop people from stealing but I didn't give a shit if they stole or not. I bought little toys for myself like I was a child. Finally, I went to a jeweller's and pawn shop run by a sweet old couple and pierced ears and noses with little guns. I was good at it, fast and friendly. On bank holidays I did thirty maybe forty pairs of ears in a day.

I was still bleeding from my abortion when I got on the plane to Boston. I'd never been on a plane before and was amazed by the little package of socks and tiny toothpaste. I watched films and worried about whether or not the food they kept giving me was free.

That summer I would look after thirty five-year-olds during a tornado warning, leading them carefully, if not calmly, to the blacked-out canteen while trees crashed down behind us. I would walk fifteen minutes through the woods each night to the outdoor toilet hoaching with spiders. I would go and stay with other counsellors' families on farms where we'd kayak on their lake and eat corn picked that day. I'd make friends with weird, fragile kids like me. I'd travel to New York and wander around Chelsea stopping to drink coffee out of giant mugs, just like in *Friends*. Except for two illicit wine coolers I'd drink nothing for three months. I'd cry a lot in private. Eventually I stopped bleeding.

But of all the things that summer gave me what I will never forget is taking off and landing. That feeling of being lifted up and away, right in your belly. And while you're in the air you know there is nothing particularly good or bad that can happen. You're just there, in that space, headed towards something new, a small thing in the big blue sky.

23
Great Yarmouth
2018

It's a long, long coach journey from Liverpool to Great Yarmouth via London but it made sense that I would arrive at my last destination travel-beaten and nauseous just as I had all those other journeys of my youth. Besides, I had left this one until the very last possible date and had all but run out of money to pay for travel and accommodation.

Of all the places I'd return to, Great Yarmouth was the one I feared most because, honestly, I didn't feel that much different from the eighteen-year-old who had left there as if running for her life. I was scared that everything that had made living there hard when I was a teen would still have the power to undo and undermine me now.

When I had changed coach at Victoria Station I stood in line behind a woman, perhaps in her seventies, with a floral walking stick and a pink rucksack, struggling with her case, also pink. I tapped her on the shoulder.

'Are you OK there? Can I give you a hand?'

'Oh no, I'm fine. I just hope he'll let me on.'

'I think you'll be fine, you don't look like a troublemaker.'

'I've always been a rebel.'

'What are you off to do?'

'I'm visiting my niece. I'm very close to her. I went earlier this year but my daughter got sick and then died. So, I didn't want to see anyone. I just wanted to be by myself.'

'I'm so sorry. Sorry for your loss.'

She was smiling and crying at the same time as she told me that her daughter had got married in the hospital in her nightie. That they had a lovely album of the wedding full of photos 'all taken on a mobile phone, imagine!' She told me it was all organised in forty-eight hours and that they did it early enough, so her daughter could remember it all, before she got really bad at the end. As we were stepping onto the coach I told her I was sorry again.

'Well, you can't change these things.'

'No, it's true. I'm sorry anyway.'

We sat separately on the coach and said goodbye when she reached Norwich. She was such a gentle, kind soul but, somehow, she had made me feel brave. Here I was chasing my past, trying to piece things together but perhaps the real courage was in simply accepting the things that happen and learning to live with them.

We pulled into Great Yarmouth past the Wetherspoon's and I walked by the bus stop where once I had drunkenly danced in the rain in my bra and the KFC where I watched a male friend of mine get headbutted while we ate our chicken.

I pulled my wheelie suitcase down Regent Road, an artery of rock shops, Greek restaurants and a famously terrifying waxwork factory, towards the pier. I had so many memories from this road, piercing ears in one of the shops, eating cream cakes with Mum at La Continental (which passed for fancy on that street), befriending the man who stood with a giant yellow python coiled around him as I walked my arse-swishing walk to whatever waitressing job I had at the time.

It was out of season and quiet but the people who were on Regent Road – a guy on a mobility scooter holding a can of lager, a couple rowing intensely outside a pub that even when I was seventeen I didn't go into – stared at me as I walked by. Assessing,

I suppose, what I might be there for, what I was worth. I noticed that the men just stared at me openly and I walked a little faster.

On my way up the seafront I remembered the old man in a flat cap who you would always see walking his greyhound on a red lead along that stretch. I used to stop and stroke the dog and sometimes have a little chat with him. One day he had a new greyhound and told me that some boy racers had sped their car up the kerb and deliberately hit and killed the original dog while he was still holding the lead. He didn't even seem that shocked as he told me. I'd wondered what else he'd seen in his life for that not to be shocking.

As I walked along, trying to discern the sound of waves under the blare and ding of the endless line of amusement arcades, I thought hopefully that I might see him and his greyhound again. Then I remembered that it was twenty years later and he would be long dead. For a moment I was filled with loss even though I'd never even known his name.

My hotel was opposite the model village and about ten minutes from my old home on the Barracks Estate. It wasn't a nice hotel, it was cheap even by Great Yarmouth's depreciating standards, but it was spotless and warm. As my room key was slid across the check-in desk I was told it was only me and a coachful of pensioners and, sure enough, I heard the pitch and fall of their night's entertainment – a pub quiz – vibrating up through my mint-green carpet. Outside my window there was an incongruous small kidney-shaped swimming pool, like a down-and-out motel in Las Vegas.

That night I went to one of the cafes I used to work at for dinner, a greasy spoon with Formica tables at the very end of the front. For £2 an hour I used to stand at the counter and make drinks and take money wearing a red tabard and matching baseball hat while singing along to 'Waterloo Sunset' on the radio.

It hadn't changed at all except that it used to do a good trade and now it was just me and two old men sitting alone at opposite ends of the cafe ploughing through their huge plates of food. At the counter I ordered what I always had for lunch when I worked there: tea, sausage and chips and two sachets of ketchup.

The girl at the counter, with her ponytail, braces on her teeth and elaborate pink-tipped manicure, stood exactly where I had stood and used the same huge hot-water urn to make my tea. I felt so tender towards her. I wanted to tell her to be careful, that she should know there was more ahead than that cafe and nights out drinking. Instead I paid and told her I used to do her job twenty years earlier.

She called in the owner who had been sitting outside and he told me he'd bought it from the children of the Greek owners I'd worked for. He said the mum was very sick but the dad was still well enough.

'That's because she worked so hard. Did they go back to Greece? She always told me when they retired they'd go back.'

He laughed. 'Nah, when you're in Great Yarmouth you never get to leave it.'

As we talked a fluorescent insect catcher rat-tat-tatted out a fly massacre.

When my sausage and chips arrived I dotted them with ketchup just as meticulously as my seventeen-year-old self had.

They tasted like shit but the experience was a good one otherwise.

Back at the hotel I walked into the bar as the lounge singer was singing 'Save the Last Dance for Me'. I ordered a half of lager and lime while scanning the room. All those pensioners, drinking their tiny glasses of drink, entirely motionless and expressionless, as the singer gave it his all.

I drank my lager and lime in my single bed and then fell sleep to the final strains of 'Green, Green Grass of Home'.

In the morning I walked past Jurassic World, Norfolk's lamest tourism attraction (quite an achievement), with its plastic dinosaurs and on to the Pleasure Beach. Though the gates were open there wasn't a soul around and I wandered among the Snail Ride, the carousel, the hall of mirrors and several giant fibreglass ice-cream cones, all alone. There was still a vague phantom smell of chips and candyfloss.

It was eerie but also a little thrilling to be there when it was silent, to have it all to myself when I'd grown up listening to its mechanical and tourist screams.

Through a gap in a gate I saw the street where I was raped. Of course, I knew it was there. I turned away from it and I got a fright from the ghost-house Lurch, lying in wait by the ticket booth. I yelped and then laughed at myself.

I didn't even think about it before I walked across to the cul-de-sac and tried to work out which house it had been. But I couldn't remember beyond it being one on the left-hand side. Still, I stood in front of those houses, feeling, well, nothing really. Except, maybe, strong. Except, maybe, genuinely, finally over it. There was nothing to be afraid of. Nothing in this town, not even that night, had bent or bucked or broken me permanently. Nothing before it had either. I'd made fucking lemonade.

I walked to my old street via a side alley. I hadn't realised before how close I'd lived to that other house. Only minutes away. My old council house had the exact same red door, now sun-faded to a rosy pink, but Mum's beloved pampas grass was gone. I took some pictures and thought about leaving but something made me approach the door. Before I could knock a guy of about forty, with a skinhead and nice way about him, was staring at me like he'd been expecting me.

'Hiya.'

'Hi, sorry, I was just wondering if I could take a picture of the front. I used to live here twenty years ago.'

'We moved in nineteen years ago. We got it in exchange for our place on King Street.'

'Yeah, that was my mum! Short Scottish woman?'

'Did you draw a big picture of an eyeball in the bedroom with "I C U" written around it?' He wrote the letters in the air with his fingers. I'd forgotten about that.

'Yes, God, sorry. What a creepy kid.'

'You want to come inside then?'

And so I did.

Inside, the house was much nicer than it had been, lots of care had been put into decorating it. But the size of the living room, so small you could only fit a chair and a sofa in it, was shocking, even to me who'd lived in London flats for fourteen years. He introduced me to his wife, who sat in the armchair under a fleece blanket, and then went off to make me a tea.

We smiled at each other. It turned out we were the same age but hadn't known each other. 'Sorry, I don't want to disturb you if you're not feeling well. You must be wondering what he's doing, inviting in a stranger off the street!'

'No, I'm not sick. Just tired.'

She explained that she got up at 3 a.m. to clean caravans at the local Haven Holiday Park.

'The house is lovely now. It must have been bare bones when you moved in.'

'The first week we moved in I called my dad and said, "Please, please come do my living room."'

We laughed, and I said gently, so she wouldn't think I was offended, 'I know. We just didn't have any money. We were doing our best.'

Her husband came through then and offered to show me the work he'd done on the bathroom. He proudly showed me their new shower, their proper washing machine.

'Can you still hear the roller coaster in here?'

'Yeah –' he made the noise of it climbing to its peak – 'tchk, tchk, tchk . . .'

'When you're taking a piss?'

'Yeah.'

As I drank my tea they told me about their three kids. She'd had her first when she was nineteen. Like me, they'd all gone to Caister High School, 'so as not to spend time with the estate kids'. One was working for his grandad, she said, one was doing A levels, but the youngest one, a fourteen-year-old, who they thought was autistic but didn't want her to be labelled as such, had been permanently expelled. While she spoke she gestured to framed pictures on the wall behind me of them dressed up to look like they were in a Western saloon. Her husband added a sentence here or there in that easy way long-married couples do.

'I hate these things – give you cancer!'

She turned to me. 'He means the air-freshener.'

I looked at the innocuous Ambi Pur sitting on the shelf.

'What I love is that when he said that he was holding a fag,' she added.

We all bellowed. I finished my tea and thanked them. 'It's been really fucking weird to be back but it was so kind of you to invite me in.' It had been somehow relaxing, fun even, to sit there with them with our shared history and understanding. I had been welcomed in so easily. She had been so warm, so calm and seemed genuinely happy and contented.

It occurred to me that her life was the one I had been avoiding, the one I was desperately scared of having, but, actually, the way she wore it, it didn't seem like a bad thing at all despite the hardships.

After leaving their house I walked through the estate and towards King Street. It was a walk I'd done so many times, in the daytime with college folders, or at night in high heels, full of cheap booze and the possibility of excitement. I overheard two women having a gossip.

'I heard he's on smack now.'

'He's on crack. Everyone's saying it's my fault but it's not my fault.'

'I can see your tears for him.' Her voice was loaded with sarcasm.

'Yeah, look really, really closely.'

'Under a microscope you'll see them.'

I walked past a massage parlour, amazed a brothel I remembered from my teens was still in business. The notice in the window marked it out as one of the few places hiring.

As I approached King Street, which in my time had been a long string of nightclubs, I remembered that everyone I spoke to in passing had said to me I wouldn't recognise it. 'We call it little Portugal,' they said. 'You won't hear anyone speak English on that road.' I walked past Polish supermarkets, Portuguese cafes, there were plenty of people from many different communities and this comforted me; perhaps things in this small town, that I'd remembered as so closed off from the rest of the world in every way, were changing for the better.

Sitting outside a cafe full of people drinking espresso and tiny bottles of beer while playing cards, so reminiscent of a Lisbon cafe that I felt the spin of dissociation, were three men. Holding out my hand and telling them I was a writer, I asked their opinion of Great Yarmouth.

They looked at me with amusement but also treated me politely, each shaking my hand. One was every bit the European in smart suede loafers and pink shirt; another, who introduced himself as the owner of the cafe, was short, stocky, perhaps a little cocky. The third was a bear of a man in an apron sporting a yellow-brown, almost healed black eye.

The owner told me they were Egyptian and Turkish. We talked briefly about Istanbul and I told them how happy it made me to see these new businesses. 'This was all clubs and pubs when I lived here.'

I asked how the local community had responded to the new businesses and the owner shook his head and gestured around. 'The council don't want to help us. I wanted to put out more chairs outside and they fined me.' He told me he'd wanted to put on live music in the evening, that he'd paid all of his licences, 'and still the council wanted another £1,000 . . . almost like they want to kill the small business. They're trying to squeeze us out.'

The man with the black eye said he had to get back to work. 'Writer, you sit here.' He gestured to his vacated seat and I sat down to speak with the man in the pink shirt. I asked him how he found living in the area. He explained he'd moved to London thirty years ago from Turkey, he'd started off cleaning a restaurant, then worked as a waiter and finally he trained as a chef. His children were living in a house he owned in London. He came to Great Yarmouth in 1999 and opened a traditional Turkish restaurant in Gorleston.

His manner was charming, perhaps even a little flirtatious,

but his anger was clear. 'The issue is, I didn't come take their jobs. I created jobs, I *made* jobs . . . I'm not saying all of them, but a lot of them, they're on benefits. And they don't have to do anything. They just get money. They get £300–400 a week.'

This wasn't true of my own experience or for many people close to me so I made a non-committal noise. 'Yes, but do you think there's enough work, here in Great Yarmouth?' I was trying to broach the many reasons why people might not be able to work or find themselves trapped in the benefits system.

'If people want to work they'll find a way.' He went on to say that the turkey factories (the only guaranteed work for young people even when I was a teen) were filled with Lithuanian and Polish workers. 'I'm not saying that all English people are lazy but most of them are.' I didn't tell him I would rather do almost anything else than go and work in a turkey-processing factory myself.

I asked, who was using these new bars and cafes, was there trouble like there used to be?

'They're 70% Portuguese.' He moved his head from side to side while weighing up his estimate. 'Here, let me get you a coffee.'

'Oh, no thanks, really I'm fine.'

'I'll pay.'

'That's kind, but really, I'm OK. I should be heading off now anyway.'

We shook hands again. He had been nice, charismatic even, but it was a long time since I'd spoken to someone incredibly conservative and not challenged them on their views. But it didn't feel right to somehow. What did I know about his experience or his life here? I was just a visitor.

I did walk away wondering if he would have been so open, offering me that coffee, if he'd known I was once one of those lazy benefits scroungers doing nothing and declining to gut factory-farmed turkeys for minimum wage and minimum respect. I left with the uneasy knowledge of that hostility and fragmentation.

On the way back into town, I passed an alley that led towards my old friend Lisa's block. Sitting on the low wall there was a group of drinkers, male and female, old and young, drinking cans of cider. I said hello and they said hello, I smiled, it was friendly enough, but it made my heart sore. Each of them, I knew, would have a story, would have hopes and people they loved and things they still thought they might do with their lives. I walked on wishing that at least a few of them would get to do those things.

Further up the street were echoes of the person I'd been before. There was the pub where I danced on the pool table show-ing my gusset to the men below, there was the bar which had always been empty and probably still was even though it did £1.60 doubles. And the club-wear shop where, when I was flush, I'd buy tiny Lycra dresses with so many holes cut out they were barely dresses at all.

I saw a sign for Harbour Community Radio in an old shop-front and went in to ask if there was anyone I could talk to about their work. An older woman, who I'd later find out also grew up on the Barracks, and a middle-aged rocker told me it was Nev I wanted. 'Nev's the man,' said the rocker solemnly, 'but he's very busy.' I told them I'd try my luck in an hour. They said again, 'He's a very busy man though.'

Further up King Street where Prism Records used to be was a shop full of second-hand furniture and a sign that said Jan's Junk Shack. It looked like my kind of place so I went in. A black guy in his fifties wearing a floral bandana smiled and welcomed me in, introducing himself as Gino.

Inside there was a work table, tools, a row of sewing machines and items of furniture in various stages of repurposing. A woman, also in her fifties, was sanding down a mirror frame. She was friendly, her pale eyes watering as she told me she was Jan, and this was her shack. Her long grey hair was adorned with a handwoven golden hairband. She explained that this was a community space where people could come and do crafts. I said I was writing a book about my youth and when I thought of Great Yarmouth I always thought of a place where you might as well get wrecked because there was nothing, really nothing, better to do.

At the work table, a teenager had kicked off her combat boots to work the sewing machine in socked feet. She was making aprons repurposed from duvet covers. They definitely still looked like duvet covers but it was a neat idea and I said so. Gino asked me where I was living and when I said Liverpool he told me that was his football team and he dreamed of going to see them play.

Amazed by my good luck I asked Jan if she had a minute to talk to me and though she said she wasn't sure what she could tell me she kept chatting and sanding anyway.

'I'm trying to get a sense of whether things are better. I understand there are a lot of community organisations here, but they're doing it all on their own. A lot of time, a lot of effort, a lot of doing it under their own steam.'

'Yes, and I volunteer. I volunteer all my services.'

Gino came over to offer a cup of tea and there was much back and forth as I refused and they all insisted, with Jan telling me it was one of the things they did, 'coffee, tea and biscuits'. The teenager shouted out 'Ah you . . . bummer' as she broke her needle and Jan reassured her they had plenty more.

We laughed. Jan returned to sanding. 'This is part of Community that Works – they do projects around here. A year ago, if you'd seen me, I was very quiet and subdued – I'm like a different person since being involved with them. Then I got an offer to run this place. So, within a short time, just five weeks ago, it was all set up. Every day at 10.30 I'm here . . . It's therapeutic and somewhere to go. Keeps everyone off the streets. And happy. We get donations of bits along the way and beg and plead. But it's not been in the paper at all yet.'

'And is this provided by the council?'

'It's called a free space. If someone decides they want to rent it, then we'll have a month's notice to empty everything out and move on.'

But, she added, it could be up to five years until someone might be interested in letting it commercially again.

Outside the shop door, Gino played his guitar and whistled and we both stopped and smiled for a moment. 'You can tell when he's coming cos you can hear him playing up the street.'

She told me the street was scary at night and Gino came to make sure she didn't get any trouble. It was funny, I said, that Great Yarmouth hadn't changed in all these years.

'Yes,' she agreed, 'it's stood still since we moved here twenty years ago.'

As I left I told her how much I would have loved that shop when I was a teen and going right off the rails. I would have loved Jan too with her soft voice and slow patience. And Gino with music preceding him wherever he went. I hoped they'd get their five years and that perhaps some young people would take a chance and wander in, bored and maybe lonely, and find a place where they wouldn't have to fight or put on a front for a few hours. In the meantime, I was glad for the teenager sitting there in her stockinged feet at a sewing machine, drinking tea with Jan and Gino.

*

You can say many things about Great Yarmouth but their chip stalls on the market are genuinely excellent and that also hadn't changed. A woman queuing with her son turned to me as we watched the server ladle a mound of chips into a paper cone and put an ice-cream-scoop-size dollop of garlic mayonnaise on top. 'This is just the potato course of our dinner.'

'Same for me. Just a light snack.'

Behind me I noticed a young girl in DMs, with pink hair, wearing a Doors T-shirt, holding a sketchbook to her chest. She could have been me.

Sitting on a bench to eat my chips, gimlet-eyed seagulls the size of puppies started to surround me. I caught another woman's eye. 'It's very intimidating.'

'It is. They're big, aren't they?'

'Yeah, it's because they're living on chips!'

As I stood, they started a cawing chorus, one after the other calling for me. As if I owed them something.

I walked down The Lanes and noticed the Yarmouth Market Cafe was still rocking a fifties decor, no signs of wear and tear at all, and that the biggest and busiest shop was, implausibly, the New Age kind that sells dream catchers and crystals. If I'd kept going in that direction I would have reached Dick Van Dykes, a gay bar that did lock-ins, where I drank double vodka and Cokes with tiny penis ice cubes floating about in them and kissed girls lustily in the toilet cubicles after dancing to Abba all night. Instead, I took a left and walked by the old post office, now turned into flats, that me and Mum queued outside on a Monday with everyone else before it opened, impatiently thinking about the tea and cake we'd have as soon as the benefits book was cashed after a weekend of no treats and sometimes very little food. The memory immediately made me want to go and eat something sweet, simply because I could, so I went and bought a Cadbury's Whole Nut bar and demolished it in three clean bites.

I passed a UKIP office. It was one of the few new enterprises in the town. Great Yarmouth was one of the biggest supporters of leaving the European Union in the country, with 71.5% voting for Brexit. I noted that they were meant to be open until 5.30 but were already closed by 4.45 with no explanation as to why. Who was supposed to be work-shy again?

Around the corner I was sure I saw my stepdad and stopped for a second in fright. I knew there was a chance of bumping into him but, until that moment, when I saw the big beer belly, blond-grey curls, the hard stare from across the road, I'd thought it was unlikely. Keep walking, I told myself. But when I looked back I realised he couldn't possibly have been my stepdad – he was probably the age Richie was when we first met. I supposed he was just aggressively assessing me for sex and I briefly considered going over to him and asking if he'd want someone looking at his mum, sister or daughter that way.

Returning to Harbour Radio, Nev was now back. Stylishly dressed and confident, almost to the point of flamboyance, he reminded me of someone in the music business, which I suppose he was.

I asked him what he thought about the town. He told me he'd been living there for thirty years. 'I couldn't understand why people were very negative. It frustrated me. We decided when we made the application for the radio that we'd highlight the positive . . . one of my own gripes, if you'll beg my pardon, is I am high into getting more people to study more history. About Great Yarmouth.'

He said he wanted it to be the new Margate.

'There's a fair balance between people who've grown up here

and those who have immigrated here. Like me. When I came here I loved it. You know, the girls were quirky. And because they'd never go anywhere, never go *anywhere*, they loved this chocolate-coloured guy and I thought that was fabulous. I thought, hey, this is easy.'

I laughed and then we talked about the possibilities for Great Yarmouth. 'What's heartbreaking,' I said, 'is that, coming back, you can see the potential.'

'Yes, if people just learned to look at the town through a different set of eyes. The radio shows that helped to put me on the map were all about me saying that people didn't understand the town they were living in.'

He said he drove people around Sheffield, Huddersfield, Harrogate, Newcastle and Middlesbrough. His aim was to give people an insight into where else they might be living.

'What's made it hard now is Brexit. And it's just gone crazy, I was so upset that day cos I was a Remainer. I'm a man in my mid-fifties, what else do I know? I was brought up as a European.'

'Yeah, there's so much more diversity now. It's noticeable.'

'When I first came here I only met two, maybe three black geezers. But now . . . it's the same all over the UK. There's no more segregated areas. There's no more "normal for Norfolk" any more. That doesn't exist. I've lived here longer than I've lived anywhere else . . . I just wonder what's going to happen in six months.'

'What's going to happen to these new businesses?'

'They're going home. The guy next door sent me a mail saying sorry I didn't get to say goodbye, we've all gone back to Angola, we're all scared . . . and you're thinking, oh my God, what's happening? But I'm not Jesus, I can't do anything about it. All I can do is just keep bigging Great Yarmouth up.'

I asked him what he thought the future might be like for the town.

'We'll see. I think we'll win.'

I told him I'd taken up enough of his time, thanked him and said I'd start listening to the shows. He led me down to the basement where he proudly showed off a state-of-the-art recording studio. Back in the shopfront area Nev said he'd expect a copy of my book in the post, and the rocker said, 'It's all him, you know. Nev's the man.' And Nev laughed modestly, said they were all a team, and showed me out.

Though I didn't share his enthusiasm for Great Yarmouth I'd been impressed by his will, and him putting it where his mouth was, to change things. And I felt he was right about a lot of it, there were things about the town that could be developed, that could be exploited, 360 days a year. Great Yarmouth, it seemed, was intent on trying to flog a seaside horse, donkey if you like, but the town needed to change and adapt to survive. Embracing the new Portuguese and Turkish population might have been a start – after all, the majority of seafront restaurants had been owned and run successfully by Greek immigrants – and focusing on creating a different sort of town that wasn't just booze, transient cheap thrills and shady landlords. But with children's centres closing, the UKIP office front and centre of the main shopping area, and the local government apparently intent on denying the new diverse, skilled community an opportunity to thrive, let alone help shape the town's future, I couldn't say I shared Nev's optimism.

Later, eating a pizza in a pub I used to get blind drunk in, a woman in a parka smiled over at me. 'Can I close this window?'

'Sure, lovely, I'm cold too.'

I busied myself with my dinner while the man she was with kept trying to explain some sort of complicated three beers for £5 deal to her until she turned back to me. 'We went to school together.'

I didn't recognise her at all. 'Maybe.'

'Caister?'

'Yeah, that's right, but I'm sorry I don't remember your face.'

'Tara Hammond?'

She was slimmer and paler than she had been; I'd forgotten that though the town might have stayed frozen in time people still aged.

'Of course. Wow.'

'We were in drama together. We did that play, *The Terrible Fate of Humpty Dumpty*?'

'I don't remember. Who was the drama teacher again?'

'Mrs Sullivan.'

'She did the robot at every school disco!'

I remembered Tara had left school to have a kid and asked how he was doing. She told me he was working for his dad but she didn't seem happy about it. I told her I was back to do some research for a book I was writing. 'What are you doing now?'

'Nothing.'

I thought she would continue – 'Nothing . . . just . . .' – and waited, but the silence stretched out over the sticky tables.

'Nothing?'

It was a stupid thing to ask and I regretted it. But I was surprised. She'd always been bright, she taught me what a double negative was. She looked embarrassed and shook her head. I started nervously gabbling about how the town hadn't changed but it was so much quieter and she explained the shops had moved outside so if you didn't have a car you couldn't get to them. We said our goodbyes with vague promises to look each other up on Facebook that neither of us followed up on.

I did remember *The Terrible Fate of Humpty Dumpty*, and I also remembered we'd argued during rehearsals. I remembered then, too, that she'd caught me working in a pub while claiming Jobseeker's (she was working at the jobcentre at the time) but had never grassed me up and I regretted not saying thank you.

I went to the Pier Head pub for a half of lager and to write up some notes. It was deserted except for a lone pensioner in a white tracksuit who looked a little like Jimmy Savile. Until a gang of twenty northern blokes on a stag do turned up and started waving their dicks around. It was actually just one dick but that's enough really. I left amazed how quickly you adapt to places, or perhaps reassimilate. That when that guy got his dick out at the next table, I just finished my half, put away my notebook and left. That I walked the same streets that had made me nervy with a new sense of ownership and purpose, knowing that if anyone gave out to me, I would give it right back.

Before I returned to my tiny hotel room, I walked around the arcades, looking like the saddest tourist ever, and played a few rounds on the 2p machines for old times' sake. I walked through the most Las Vegas of all arcades to the quiet end of the pier. Sitting in the darkness on a picnic bench sat two teenage boys, listening to AJ Tracey on one of their phones. I walked over and introduced myself. 'How do you feel about growing up here?'

Jack, the slighter of the two, a little pimply, with his fringe brushed over his eyes answered first. 'It's all right. It's not as bad as people make it out to be, yeah . . . at school everyone's like "oh, you live in Yarmouth . . . blah, blah, blah".'

Did they feel there were enough opportunities for them? 'Yeah, yeah, especially in summer. You want a job you can get one.'

Callum, his friend, had the look of a well-fed country lad. 'To be fair, I find it difficult to get here. The buses are rubbish and they stop at like six.' He lived in one of the tiny satellite villages.

I asked them if they'd want to stay here. Callum replied that he wanted to live in the countryside but Jack said, 'I like it here. I've got a moped. So if I want to go somewhere, like see him in a village, I can. Here there's loads of stuff to do and I've got a job so –'

'What's your job? Do you mind me asking?'

'I work in a corner shop, so it's not very much but, yeah . . .'

He suddenly seemed so young I wanted to reassure him he was doing OK. 'That's good. That's a lot more than a lot of people have in the UK at the moment. When I was growing up here I found it pretty rough. Do you find the same?'

Callum spoke up in his deep voice again. 'It still is to be fair –'

'I live in Newtown,' Jack cut in, 'around the racecourse, and that's where the posh people live. I always say, that's the good part, it starts getting a bit rough like where the clubs are and –' he gestured to my old estate – 'that bit's not too nice.'

We all laughed as I nodded and said, 'Yeah, that's fair enough.'

I thanked them and shook both their hands. Callum's handshake was bone-dry, while Jack's was cold and clammy. I wanted to soothe him. Let him know I was friendly, that he'd nothing to worry about. They turned back to their music and I left them in the darkness of the pier, the waves crashing under them.

Back at the hotel, drinking a pint of lime and soda in bed, I recorded some thoughts on my phone. Listening back, I'd be surprised by how buoyant I sounded. I laughed a lot during the recording, the muffled chords of 'Sweet Caroline' vibrating up through the hotel's floor to accompany my voice.

'It's been positive. I'm just not the same person. I've been so confident, walked up to people and asked them all sorts of questions. I haven't felt in any way intimidated. Largely because I just regained some of that swagger I developed while I was here, where you learn to assess and learn who's a threat and who isn't. And . . . I've just changed. I'm a different, new, person. And that's incredibly freeing. And that's it. I'm going to speak to my husband in a little bit.' There's a pause in the recording. 'I'm trying to remember if there's anything I've forgotten but I don't think there is. Nothing that I need to remember right now.'

24
Great Yarmouth
1999

I came back to Great Yarmouth from America after my three months. I returned plump from corn syrup and American portions, wearing jeans and T-shirts from Walmart, having barely drunk a drop while I was away. I returned hopeful and determined. After all, I had made it all the way to America so what other miracles might be possible? Somehow the house, the estate, my life as it was then seemed just what it was – small and impermanent.

Perhaps my demons might have found me once again back in my old bedroom or haunting the same sad nightclubs if it hadn't been for the college course I enrolled in. A BTEC National Diploma in Performing Arts that took place at a tiny old community theatre known as the Seagull. I was able to get the New Deal dole by saying I was learning to be a lighting technician which was considered vocational enough to qualify.

There, I was given the gift of a truly inspirational teacher. A Liverpudlian called Ian Gordon who didn't believe, like so many others did, that kids on BTECs were the stupidest of them all, only capable of working a trade. His teaching was, and perhaps still is, one of the most radically political things I have ever experienced. He did not treat art like it was something that belonged to other people. Instead, he gave it to us in all its forms, showed us how to make our own, and told us repeatedly why it was important that we, the kids from the wrong places with the hard memories, did so. He served as a proxy father to some. He refused to give up on any of us.

I decided I would achieve the highest grades I could, and

would leave the Barracks Estate early in the morning and return on the last bus. Between classes and play rehearsals we sat around in the old theatre which became a home for those of us who didn't necessarily want to return to our own. Ian helped me write my UCAS application and coached my audition piece for university. He told me I could do anything I wanted.

My audition speech was Lady Macbeth decrying the permanence of the stains of all her mistakes that could never be washed away. I got an unconditional offer to start university in London. I finally made my way to the big city that seemed to promise everything, but most of all a future with wide horizons and choices that would be mine.

From that moment onwards, I started running and didn't look back. Until this year, until I was ready.

25
Liverpool
2018

It's two nights before I'm due to send this book to my publisher. I've spent the day trying to work out how you end a book like this. Because, for me, it doesn't feel like an ending. It feels like a beginning.

This year has allowed me to answer many of the questions I've had and lay to rest falsehoods about poverty that had frequently left me feeling other or lesser. I can see now it is in many people's interest for the poor to stay poor, for the communities I came from to be made to believe they deserve nothing better, for a large proportion of society to believe that if you are poor then you are somehow undeserving of empathy. That, somehow, poverty is a personal choice or failing, and had you only worked hard enough, you might have avoided the fate of daily, unrelenting hardship. We see these beliefs reflected across the media, from the way shaming the poor has become routine to the apocryphal idea that we live in a meritocracy.

It doesn't take much to unpack this though, to acknowledge that we exist in a society where, from the very earliest age, your income affects everything, from your likelihood of mental illness or substance abuse to domestic violence, low educational attainment, even the number of metal fillings in your teeth. If we admit this obvious imbalance, those who have not experienced those disadvantages would have to accept the relative privilege they have enjoyed and act to change things.

First in line here must surely be a hostile government who, in the last eight years of austerity, has sought to take from those who can least afford it, to trim fat where there was only bone in the first place, while offering tax cuts for the wealthy. The result? We live in the world's sixth-richest economy but one-fifth of us live in poverty. Local councils in England have seen a 49% reduction in government funding since 2010–11. Five hundred children's centres have been closed in the past eight years and more than 340 libraries closed between 2010 and 2016, with the accompanying loss of 8,000 library jobs. These statistics promise yet more families who won't be given the chance to return to work or, if they do, who will be forced into zero-hour contracts that will barely feed their families. They mean even less of a chance to make a better life, access mental health support or live in stable housing. More children who will continue growing up in great difficulty with no hope of reprieve – the Institute for Fiscal Studies predicts a rise of 7% in child poverty between 2015 and 2022 – all while being told that somehow their parents, and they themselves, are to blame. And it's not just the poor of today who will suffer because, as I know only too well, poverty seeps down the generations, hardship is passed down the bloodline. Simply put, this government paid for tax breaks for the wealthy with our children's futures and, somehow, we allowed them to.

When I think of the obstacles to class equality in this country, to trying to make changes, it can feel impossible. How can my chipping away change anything? But then I remember Sally and her colleagues, Bill, Jan, Nev and the countless others working in communities, finding solutions that actually work because they've been there themselves. Each of them simply recognising a need and doing what they can.

I have my own balances to settle for the good life I've been given. I'll start by using all I've learned in writing this book. I will never let lazy assumptions about what it means to be poor, or how poverty happens, pass. I will support grass-roots groups plugging the holes in the welfare state tirelessly and effectively, campaigning against this war on the poor that is happening right now on our streets and in our cities.

It's my hope that readers of this book might decide to do the same. If we all chip away, person by person, doing what we can, with enough of us, I believe it is possible to change the future.

This book has already changed my future forever. I now have some family again – an aunt, an uncle, cousins and second cousins. They like my Facebook posts occasionally and in the mornings I eat my toast with jam made by my Aunt Allie. One of my second cousins sends me beautiful, lyrical messages about his life climbing mountains and exploring Buddhism.

They all send me anecdotes of my childhood and photos of me looking mucky and fat-faced. Reuniting me with someone I thought I'd lost forever. They know I don't speak to my mum, and why, and respect that. They treat me with warmth, kindness and decency. There are boundaries and they are never breached. No one calls each other names. I never imagined such a thing might happen within my family or that I might use the term 'my family' affectionately and with attachment again.

Peter and I have been trying for a baby for a few months now. Each month I am sure I can feel the growing of a new life inside of me and I feel only joy and hope for being a parent and bringing up a child. I think I'll be a good mother.

In retracing the lines that held me to the path of the past, I've freed myself from so much shame and fear. The child I was still walks beside me but now I know how to care for her. Just as I will my own child, biological, fostered or adopted, using everything I've been taught about what love is. And what love is not.

It's late and I'm home alone. I'm trying to call Susan, my mum's cousin, who I haven't spoken to in thirty-three years. She used to look after me when she was fourteen and I was a newborn. I was her flower girl though I've no recollection of it. She picks up. 'My God, you sound . . . so Aberdonian. I mean, you would, but still.'

What I actually mean is that she has the same voice as the women of my family, lilting and soporific, never to be hurried unless they worked themselves up into a rage. It is like speaking to a part of me that has been buried deep until this moment.

Susan, whose mother was my grandma's sister, is a social worker in Aberdeen now. She was in care for most of her teens, left school without any qualifications, and then had four kids before retaking her Scottish Leaving Certificate, having another child, and then training as a social worker. She talks me through our family tree. The mental illness, the alcoholism, the fights. I ask a lot of questions. Most of what I assumed she confirms. I learn some new startling facts about just how entrenched the psychosis, physical and verbal abuse ran within the previous generations. But that's done now, she says.

'Our generation, the ones that are left –' suicide also runs in the family – 'we all get on now.'

When we come to a lull I ask the question I've most wanted to, about my stays in foster homes and why they happened. The piece of the puzzle that is missing but that I felt would help me understand everything else.

'Now, I'm also going to tell you this. I think you deserve to know. You were three at the time and my brother Craig, he had mental health problems, you wouldn't leave him with a kid. He came to me with you crying saying, "Her mum asked me to look after her for a few hours and she hasn't been back for three days." You were crying, filthy, starving. You were just this little child that wasn't getting looked after, Kerry. And it was bad, you know, you were so distressed at that point. He'd been wandering about not knowing what to do, he didn't know to change you, you were cold and dirty, he had no food to feed you.'

I remember the fear of that night with Peter in that room in Vietnam. The frightened crying child I became because I didn't know what had happened to me, just that there was a big, terrifying, black hole.

'Oh God. God.'

'You were just a tiny child. You didn't even get a few years' good start.'

For a moment we're both silent and I'm wondering if she's fighting back the tears like I am. But mine aren't tears of sadness, they're tears of relief. Because that is the truth. And all my life I've needed someone, one of my own, to simply tell me that honestly.

'I'm so glad you're putting this all down. You're writing, that's therapeutic.'

'Yeah, I've been writing it for a year now and it's been so hard. I'm handing it in this week and it'll be done. You know, the whole time I've been tearing myself in two because I'm so desperate to know about this stuff, and the more I know, the more I'll be able to process and put things into context, but it hasn't been easy.' I pause.

'But you can't think about it, Kerry. At the end of the day, this is your life. This was your experience. And our parents made choices and those choices had an impact on their children. You as a human being in your own right have a right to your experiences.

You're not writing what's not true.' And, again, it's as though she's been sent to say the very thing I most needed to hear, spoken in the voice of my blood and my foremothers. 'It's brilliant you've put it all into writing. It's great to see that you've come through all of that and you've a good life, Kerry. I'm so happy about that.'

'Yeah, I really do. My husband, you'll have to meet him at some point, is the nicest man in the world and we're trying for a baby at the moment.'

'Ach!'

'Well, I'm thirty-eight now so I hope I haven't left it too late but it seems if I've learned anything it's that we're good at making babies in our family.'

'Aye, fighting, drinking and babies!'

'Well, I'll stick to babies then.'

We end the call still laughing with promises to meet soon.

Later Peter and I sit on our gently stained £50 sofa eating fish and chips as I tell him all the things I learned during the call, which lasted just over an hour but which had shifted and settled so much for me.

'So, imagine, all that schizophrenia and bipolar and all that drink and drugs. It's no wonder.'

I tell him about one of Grandma's relatives throwing a crystal ashtray at her own brother's head in a fairly low-level domestic row and splitting his face right open.

'You know what they used to call the Mackies on the docks? Torry Seagulls. Always begging for scraps.'

'Really?'

'They had nothing. They used to go down to try to get a few lumps of coal or some food.'

He shakes his head. 'I'm so sorry about it all.'

'It's OK. Honestly, it's in the past and I survived, a lot of us did. And look, I've you and some family and my work. I feel like a whole person. With roots and history. Like I'm fully fledged. There's a part of me that's really proud to belong to all that strength, and that after everything that happened I'm still here and not just here but happy.'

'And now you're using that strength in a different way.'

'Exactly.'

We sit and finish our fish and chips, curled up together. We talk about a trip to Aberdeen in spring, how my aunt is sending us some more jam. I talk about writing the book of my grandma and her sisters, 'The Torry Seagulls'.

On the record player Leonard Cohen sings 'That's No Way to Say Goodbye'.

But, for me, the moment is perfect.

Acknowledgements

More than any other, this book has required me to seek out people who might help me in telling the stories beyond my own. Thank you to everyone I spoke with both formally and informally – I hope you all know you not only helped me tell the stories of your communities but also allowed me to connect with a past I thought was lost forever, and I am so grateful for that generosity. Particular thanks to my new-old family for welcoming me with such open hearts. Reconnecting with you all is one of the best gifts I've ever been given.

I often think not enough credit is given to the collaborative nature of writing a book. I cannot thank my wonderful literary agent, Juliet Pickering, enough for her endless support, championing and for lending her intelligence and wisdom to me before, during and beyond the process of this book. Likewise, to Becky Hardie, my indefatigable editor at Chatto & Windus, whose razor-sharp eye, insight and real belief in the book and me were what got these pages out from inside my head and into your hands. We are all three of us coming up to ten years of work together and I couldn't wish for more astute, intelligent or kinder women to have in my corner.

Of course, there are so many more people behind the scenes who make a book. Thanks to everyone at Chatto & Windus who I am so proud to be published by, especially Clara, Charlotte and Greg for editorial support, and Sophie and Anna for helping get *Lowborn* out to the reading public. Katherine Fry had the unenviable job of copy-editing my work and I'm very grateful for her keen eye. Thank you too to Stephen Parker and Mark Vessey for a cracking book cover and author picture.

At Blake Friedmann, thank yous go to Hattie, Sam, Tom, James, Hanna, Resham, Daisy, Cassie and Emanuela, all of whom have played their part in championing this and my previous books while also being a delight to work with. A special thank you to the wonderful Isobel who has stepped into Juliet's shoes while she spends time with her mini-Pickering and made me feel in very safe hands indeed.

The *Pool's Lowborn* columns helped me write this book in ways I could never have expected – from easing me into showing my more vulnerable parts to connecting me with a reading audience who never failed to inspire and remind me why a book like this one might resonate. To the readers who messaged me to share their own stories – I hear you and I hope this book is somehow valuable to you. My eternal gratitude goes to Sam Baker and Lynn Enright for giving me that wonderful chance and the freedom to learn, and to Zoe Beatty, Cate Sevilla and all at the *Pool* for letting me continue to write about the things that are important to me/ boil my piss.

This was a challenging book to write but there were many pals, both in real life and farther afield, who helped me continue writing when things got hard even when they didn't know I needed it. Shout-outs to the #WorkingClassWriters collective and to Cathy Rentzenbrink, Kit de Waal, Nikesh Shukla, Paul McVeigh, Damian Barr, Simon Savidge for support, kind words and just 'getting it'.

As with my last two books, my bestie Levia has been by my side for cuddles, to share wine and make me laugh, and who, with Ricky, is bringing up two bright wee stars, Xander and Zarla, my godkids, who bring me more joy with each passing year.

A thank you to Liz and Werner for welcoming me into your wonderful family. Your love of books and good politics made me want to make you proud.

As you might tell from the preceding pages of this book, above all else, my life with Peter has been the thing that kept body and soul together during this strange process of picking myself apart and taking myself backwards. In a thousand small and enormous ways he has helped me write this book. I never imagined such happiness and peace could exist. Thank you, Peter. I love you so.

Resources

Citizens Advice Bureau
www.citizensadvice.org.uk
03444 111 444

Money Advice Service
www.moneyadviceservice.org.uk
0800 138 7777

Step Change Debt Charity
www.stepchange.org
0800 138 1111

Food Aid Network
www.foodaidnetwork.org.uk

The Trussell Trust
www.trusselltrust.org
01722 580 180

Shelter
www.shelter.org.uk
0808 800 4444

Centrepoint
www.centrepoint.org.uk
0333 257 5738

Crisis
www.crisis.org.uk
08000 384838

Samaritans
www.samaritans.org
116 123

Sane
www.sane.org.uk
0300 304 7000

National Domestic Violence Helpline
www.nationaldomesticviolencehelpline.org.uk
0808 2000 247

Talk to Frank
www.talktofrank.com
0300 1236600

Adfam: Families, Drugs and Alcohol
www.adfam.org.uk
020 3817 9410

Rape Crisis UK
www.rapecrisis.org.uk
0808 802 9999

NSPCC
www.nspcc.org.uk
0808 800 5000

British Pregnancy Advisory Service
www.bpas.org
03457 30 40 30